Best Easy Day Hikes
Sacramento

Help Us Keep This Guide Up to Date

Every effort has been made by the author and editors to make this guide as accurate and useful as possible. However, many things can change after a guide is published—trails are rerouted, regulations change, facilities come under new management, etc.

We would love to hear from you concerning your experiences with this guide and how you feel it could be improved and kept up to date. While we may not be able to respond to all comments and suggestions, we'll take them to heart and we'll also make certain to share them with the author. Please send your comments and suggestions to the following address:

The Globe Pequot Press
Reader Response/Editorial Department
P.O. Box 480
Guilford, CT 06437

Or you may e-mail us at:

editorial@GlobePequot.com

Thanks for your input, and happy trails!

Best Easy Day Hikes Series

Best Easy Day Hikes
Sacramento

Tracy Salcedo-Chourré

FALCONGUIDES ®

GUILFORD, CONNECTICUT
HELENA, MONTANA

AN IMPRINT OF THE GLOBE PEQUOT PRESS

FALCONGUIDES®

To buy books in quantity for corporate use
or incentives, call **(800) 962–0973**
or e-mail **premiums@GlobePequot.com**.

Maps by Offroute Inc. © Morris Book Publish-
ing, LLC

Library of Congress Cataloging-in-Publication
Data is available on file.

ISBN: 978-0-7627-5111-2

Printed in the United States of America

10 9 8 7 6 5 4 3 2 1

Contents

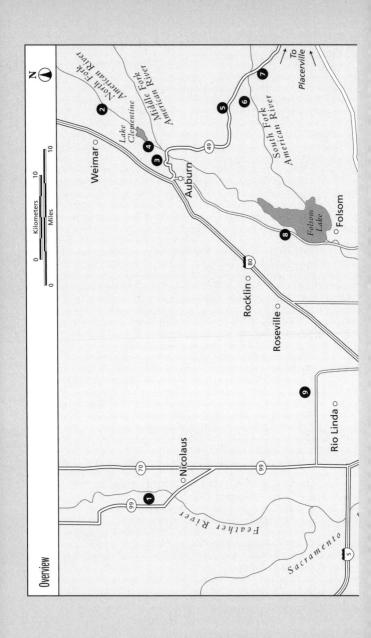

Overview

N

Kilometers
0   10

Miles
0   10

North Fork American River
Weimar
2
Lake Clementine
4
Middle Fork American River
3
Auburn
49
5
6
7
To Placerville
South Fork American River
8
Folsom Lake
Folsom
80
Rocklin
Roseville
9
Rio Linda
70
Nicolaus
99
99
Feather River
Sacramento
5

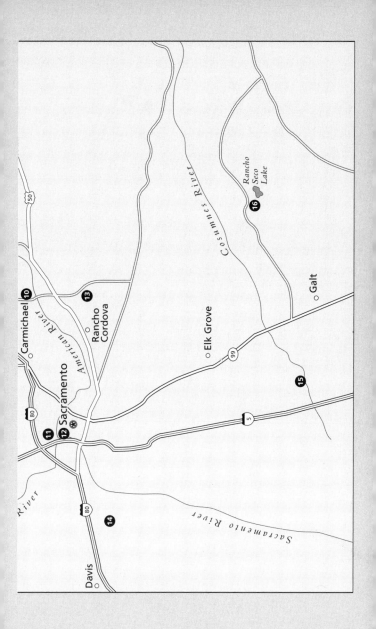

Acknowledgments

I am indebted to the lovers of wildlands that have worked over the years to preserve parks and trails throughout the Sacramento area. A guidebook like this wouldn't be possible without their efforts.

Thanks to the land managers who have taken the time to review the hikes described in this guide and to writers who have shared their impressions of and experiences on Sacramento-area trails both in books and online. Specifically I'd like to thank Mitch Sears, sustainability program manager for the City of Davis; Suzanne Bowman of Marshall Gold Discovery State Historic Park; Jeff Rhoads, outreach coordinator for the Cosumnes River Preserve; Ed Cox, bicycle and pedestrian coordinator for the city of Sacramento; Annie Parker in the county of Sacramento's communications and media office; Jill Ritzman, deputy director of Sacramento's county parks department; and Mike Lynch of Auburn State Recreation Area.

Thanks to the expert team of editors and production staff at The Globe Pequot Press for helping me make this guide the best it can be.

Thanks also to family and friends who support my work as a guidebook writer. Family is my backbone, especially my mother-in-law, Sarah; my brothers, Nick and Chris; and my parents, Jesse and Judy.

Finally, my gratitude always to my husband, Martin, and sons, Jesse, Cruz, and Penn, who never complain when I take off for the hills without them or when I drag them along. My boys are dauntless trekkers, even the youngest, Penn, who matched me mile for mile along the American River Parkway. They are unfailing supporters, and I'm very lucky to share my journey with them.

Map Legend

	Interstate Highway
	U.S. Highway
	State Highway
	Local/Forest Roads
	Unimproved Road
	Trail
	Featured Route
	Paved Trail
	River/Creek
	Intermittent Stream
	Marsh/Swamp
	Regional Park/Recreation Area
	Bridge
	Dam
	Gate
	Information/Visitor Center
	Lake or Pond
	Parking
	Peak
	Picnic Area
	Point of Interest
	Restroom
	Trailhead
	Town
	Tunnel
	Waterfall
	Viewpoint
	True North (Magnetic North is approximately 15.5° East)

Introduction

The floodplain of the Feather River stretches a good 0.5 mile from bank to bank in the Bobelaine Audubon Sanctuary. Standing at its edge, tracking the flight of a graceful white egret low over the river's riffled surface, I felt as secluded and inspired as I'd been on the banks of Alaska's remote Gerstle River.

Traversing Howard Ranch, looking east and south over great undulations of grassland, I felt small and isolated, an explorer in a lonely big-sky country where rolling prairie stretched unbroken to a curving blue horizon.

I kept having to remind myself that I was hiking less than an hour outside metropolitan Sacramento.

I'll admit it now: Sacramento trails were mostly a mystery to me before I started researching this book. I'd sampled a few in the region over the years, mostly along the American River and in the foothills, but the Central Valley was essentially a boring drive I had to endure to get from my San Francisco Bay Area home to the magnetic Sierra Nevada.

No more. Exploring Sacramento and its environs has been a revelation. I credit the great rivers for my enthusiasm, and these can't be appreciated until you stand on their banks. The Sacramento, the American, the Feather, the Cosumnes: They change in nature as they flow out of the high country and merge with one another, growing from clear, fast-moving streams that snake around rocky bars to broad, deep, navigable waterways that look lazy until the sun catches the complicated currents that churn below the surface. They support complex riparian habitats and saturate

1

wetlands that support a wealth of bird, plant, and animal life. You'll be hard-pressed to find a trail in the region that doesn't ring with birdsong.

The rivers aren't all that recommend the region's trails. Sacramento wears history like an Argonaut wears long johns—it underlies everything. Especially in the foot-hills, the fabled Gold Country, it's tough to find a trail that doesn't hearken back to California's early statehood and before. From re-creations of native Indian villages to glimpses of California's capitol building, you'll find it here.

Each hike in this guide is unique for its ecology, history, topography, or natural beauty. My intent is for these routes to serve as gateways. If the trail described here doesn't fit your needs, you can be sure another in that park or a neigh-boring open space will.

From the banks of the Feather River to the grasslands of Howard Ranch, I hope you'll find these treks as eye open-ing and satisfying as I have.

The Nature of Sacramento

Sacramento's hiking grounds range from the rugged and mountainous to the flat and paved. Hikes in this guide cover the gamut. While by definition a best easy day hike is not strenuous and generally poses little danger to the traveler, knowing a few details about the nature of the Sacramento area will enhance your explorations.

Weather

The Central Valley is blessed with a Mediterranean-type cli-mate, with rainy and dry seasons. While overall the weather is inviting, each season poses unique challenges for hikers.

The rainy season generally runs from November through

March and includes storms that can drop anywhere from a trace to several inches of precipitation. The valley lies in the rain shadow of California's Coast Ranges, so average monthly rainfall totals in winter are relatively modest, ranging from 2 to 4 inches. Average daytime high temperatures are in the 50s and 60s; average lows are in the 40s, with occasional dips into the 30s.

Winter rains may not be intimating, but the fog can be. Inversions occasionally trap moisture on the valley floor, creating dense banks of "tule" fog that can reduce visibility, in the extreme, to less than 50 feet. This poses grave dangers to travelers on area freeways and significantly limits vistas that can be enjoyed from any trail.

Conditions on some trails can degenerate into boot-sucking mud after a winter rain. A day or two of dry weather will quickly harden most surfaces so that hikers may pass easily.

In the dry season, from April through October, you'll be hard pressed for a rainy day. With hot temperatures and warm winds blowing in from the delta to the west, vegetation crisps to a crackly crunch, and hikers will crisp up too if they don't carry enough drinking water. Average daytime high temperatures range from the high 80s into the 90s, with heat waves raising the mercury into the 100s. Lows average in the 50s.

The greatest danger a hiker faces on hot summer days is dehydration. No matter the trail's length or the amount of shade along the route, carry plenty of water. When the temperatures soar, avoid hiking in the heat of the day. Morning and evening hours offer lovely light and a greater opportunity to see wildlife, as well as mitigate the risks of heat-related illness.

Critters

You'll encounter mostly benign creatures on these trails, such as deer, squirrels, rabbits, wild turkeys, and a variety of songbirds and shorebirds. More rarely seen (during the daylight hours especially) are coyotes, raccoons, and opossums. Deer in some of the parks are remarkably tame and may linger on or close to the trail as you approach.

Sacramento's parklands also are habitat for mountain lions and rattlesnakes. Signs at trailheads warn hikers if these animals might be present. Encounters are infrequent, but you should be prepared to react properly if you run across either a dangerous snake or cat. Snakes generally strike only if they are threatened. You are too big to be dinner, so they typically avoid contact with humans. Keep your distance and they will keep theirs. If you come across a cat, make yourself appear as big as possible and do not run. If you don't act like or look like prey, you stand a good chance of not being attacked.

Be Prepared

Hiking in the Sacramento Valley and Gold Country is generally safe. Still, hikers should be prepared, whether they are out for a short stroll along the Sacramento River waterfront or venturing into the secluded American River canyon at Codfish Falls. Some specific advice:

- Know the basics of first aid, including how to treat bleeding; bites and stings; and fractures, strains, or sprains. Pack a first-aid kit on each excursion.

- Familiarize yourself with the symptoms of heat exhaustion and heat stroke. Heat exhaustion symptoms include heavy sweating, muscle cramps, headache, dizziness, and fainting. Should you or any of your hiking party exhibit any of these symptoms, cool the victim down immediately by rehydrating and getting him or her to an air-conditioned location. Cold showers also help reduce body temperature. Heat stroke is much more serious: The victim may lose consciousness, and the skin is hot and dry to the touch. In this event, call 911 immediately.

- Regardless of the weather, your body needs a lot of water while hiking. A full thirty-two-ounce bottle is the minimum for these short hikes, but more is always better. Bring a full water bottle with you, whether water is available along the trail or not.

- Don't drink from streams, rivers, creeks, or lakes without treating or filtering the water first. Waterways and water bodies may host a variety of contaminants, including giardia, which can cause serious intestinal unrest.

- Prepare for extremes of both heat and cold by dressing in layers.

- Carry a backpack in which you can store extra clothing, ample drinking water and food, and whatever goodies, like guidebooks, cameras, and binoculars, you might want.

- Some area trails have cell phone coverage. Bring your device, but make sure you've turned it off or got it on the vibrate setting while hiking. There's nothing like a "wake the dead"–loud ring to startle every creature in the vicinity, including fellow hikers.

- Keep children under careful watch. The bigger rivers have dangerous currents and are not safe for swimming. Hazards along some of the trails include poison oak, uneven footing, and steep drop-offs; make sure children don't stray from the designated route. Children should carry a plastic whistle; if they become lost, they should stay in one place and blow the whistle to summon help.

Zero Impact

Trails in the Sacramento area and neighboring foothills are heavily used year-round. We, as trail users and advocates, must be especially vigilant to make sure our passage leaves no lasting mark. Here are some basic guidelines for preserving trails in the region:

- Pack out all your own trash, including biodegradable items like orange peels. You might also pack out garbage left by less considerate hikers.
- Don't approach or feed any wild creatures—the ground squirrel eyeing your snack food is best able to survive if it remains self-reliant.
- Don't pick wildflowers or gather rocks, antlers, feathers, and other treasures along the trail. Removing these items will only take away from the next hiker's experience.
- Avoid damaging trailside soils and plants by remaining on the established route. This is also a good rule of thumb for avoiding poison oak and stinging nettle, common regional trailside irritants.
- Don't cut switchbacks, which can promote erosion.
- Be courteous by not making loud noises while hiking.
- Many of these trails are multiuse, which means you'll

share them with other hikers, trail runners, mountain bikers, and equestrians. Familiarize yourself with the proper trail etiquette, yielding the trail when appropriate.

- Use outhouses at trailheads or along the trail.

Sacramento Area Boundaries and Corridors

For the purposes of this guide, hikes are confined to a one-hour drive from downtown Sacramento. The hikes reach into Sacramento, Yolo, Sutter, Placer, and El Dorado Counties and into satellite cities, including Folsom, Carmichael, Auburn, and Galt.

A number of major highways and interstates converge in Sacramento. Directions to trailheads are given from these arteries. They include Interstate 5 (north–south), Interstate 80 (east–west), U.S. Highway 50 (east–west), Highway 99 (north–south), and Highway 49 (north–south in the foothills between Auburn and Placerville).

Land Management

The following government and private organizations manage most of the public lands described in this guide and can provide further information on these hikes and other trails in their service areas:

- California State Parks, Department of Parks and Recreation, 416 Ninth Street, Sacramento 95814 (mailing address: P.O. Box 942896, Sacramento 94296); (916) 653-6995 or (800) 777-0369; www.parks.ca.gov; e-mail: info@parks.ca.gov. A complete listing of state parks is available on the Web site, along with park brochures and maps.

- Sacramento County Regional Parks Department, 3711 Branch Center Road, Sacramento 95827; (916) 875-6961; www.msa2.saccounty.net/parks; e-mail: parks info@saccounty.net. The park office is open from 8:00 a.m. to 5:00 p.m. daily.

- Bureau of Land Management, Folsom Field Office, 63 Natoma Street, Folsom 95630; (916) 985-4474; www.blm.gov or www.ca.blm.gov/folsom.

- Cosumnes River Preserve, 13501 Franklin Boulevard, Galt 95632; (916) 684-2816; www.cosumnes.org. This organization provides information about both the Cosumnes River Preserve and the Howard Ranch Trail outside Galt.

Regional trails in the area include the Jedediah Smith National Recreation Trail and the Western States Pioneer Express Recreation Trail. Portions of these trails are described in this guide. More information on the Jedediah Smith National Recreation Trail is available at www.msa2.saccounty.net/parks. For the Western States Pioneer Express Trail, visit the Western States Trail Foundation at www.teviscup.org.

Public Transportation

The Sacramento Regional Transit District offers bus and light rail service throughout the greater Sacramento metropolitan area, with service to suburban cities including North Highlands, Roseville, Folsom, Rancho Cordova, and Elk Grove. Contact information is P.O. Box 2110, Sacramento 95812-2110; (916) 321-BUSS (2877); www.sacrt.com.

How to Use This Guide

This guide is designed to be simple and easy to use. Each hike is accompanied by a map and summary information that delivers the trail's vital statistics, including a short description, the hike distance in miles and type of trail (loop or out and back), the time required for an average hiker, difficulty, the trail surface, the best season for hiking the trail, other trail users, whether dogs are allowed on the hike, applicable fees or permits, park hours, sources of additional maps, trail contacts, any special considerations you should know about, and additional trail-related information.

Directions to the trailhead are also provided, along with a general description of what you'll see along the way. A detailed route finder (Miles and Directions) sets forth mileages between significant landmarks along the trail.

Maps

The hikes in this book are easy to follow. The maps provided show each trail, so you won't need to buy extra maps. If you decide to explore farther or go off-trail, however, you'll need more detailed maps. All the hikes in this book are covered by the detailed topographic maps published by the U.S. Geological Survey (USGS)—available through local outdoors shops or by calling (888) ASK-USGS or visiting http://store.usgs.gov. If a park trail map is available, that source is also listed.

Hike Selection

This guide describes trails that are accessible to every

hiker, whether visiting from out of town or someone lucky enough to live in Sacramento. The hikes are no longer than 7 miles round-trip, and some are considerably shorter. They range in difficulty from flat excursions perfect for a family outing to more challenging treks in the foothills of the Sierra Nevada. While these trails are among the best, keep in mind that nearby trails, often in the same park or preserve, may offer options better suited to your needs.

I've sought to space hikes throughout the Sacramento area, so wherever your starting point, you'll find a great easy day hike nearby.

Difficulty Ratings

These are all easy hikes, but easy is a relative term. Some would argue that no hike involving any kind of climbing is easy, but hills are a fact of life in the Sacramento area. To aid in the selection of a hike that suits particular needs and abilities, each hike is rated easy, moderate, or more challenging. Bear in mind that even most challenging routes can be made easy by hiking within your limits and taking rests when you need them.

- **Easy** hikes are generally short and flat, taking no longer than an hour to complete.

- **Moderate** hikes involve increased distance and relatively mild changes in elevation; they will take one to two hours to complete.

- **More challenging** hikes feature some steep stretches, greater distances, and generally take longer than two hours to complete.

These are completely subjective ratings—what you think is easy is entirely dependent on your level of fitness and the adequacy of your gear (primarily shoes). If you are hiking with a group, you should select a hike with a rating that's appropriate for the least fit and prepared in your party.

Approximate hiking times are based on the assumption that most walkers average 2 miles per hour on flat ground. Adjust that rate by the steepness of the terrain and your level of fitness (subtract time if you're an aerobic animal, and add time if you're hiking with kids), and you have a ballpark hiking duration. Be sure to add more time if you plan to picnic or take part in other activities, like bird watching or photography.

Trail Finder

Best Hikes for River Lovers

Best Hikes for Lake Lovers

Best Hikes with Children

Best Hikes with Dogs

Best Hikes for Great Views

Best Hikes for Nature Lovers

Best Hikes for History Buffs

1 Bobelaine Audubon Sanctuary

Rustic paths lead through a wildlife sanctuary on the banks of the Feather River, where you'll share the trail with foxes, deer, and an entire Audubon guidebook of birds.

Distance: 4.6-mile loop

Approximate hiking time: 3 hours

Difficulty: Moderate due only to length

Trail surface: Mowed 10-foot tracks and singletrack

Best season: Winter, spring, and fall for bird watching; spring for wildflowers; fall for leaf color

Other trail users: None

Canine compatibility: Dogs not permitted

Fees and permits: No fees or permits required

Schedule: Open sunrise to sunset daily

Maps: USGS Nicolaus; Bobelaine Audubon Sanctuary map available at the preserve (when the mailbox next to the interpretive board is stocked) and online

Trail contact: Sacramento Audubon Society, P.O. Box 160694, Sacramento 95816-0694; www.sacramentoaudubon.org. Phone numbers and e-mail addresses for society officials are available on the Web site.

Special considerations: Remain on trails to avoid contact with poison oak and to protect fragile wildlife habitat.

Additional information: Trailhead amenities are minimal, consisting of parking for about ten cars, a portable toilet, and an information board. Bring drinking water. Groups of ten or more are asked to contact the Sacramento Audubon Society in advance.

Finding the trailhead: From downtown Sacramento take Interstate 5 north to the Highway 70/99 junction. Go right (north) on Highways 70/99 toward Marysville and Yuba City for 19.3 miles, staying left on Highway 99 where it diverges from Highway 70. Cross the Feather

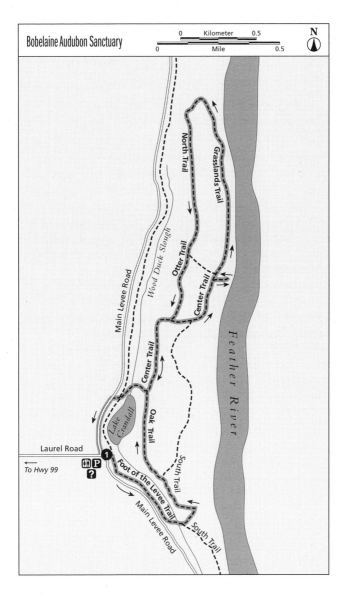

Bobelaine Audubon Sanctuary

Kilometer
0   0.5
Mile
0   0.5

N

Main Levee Road

North Trail

Grasslands Trail

Wood Duck Slough

Otter Trail

Center Trail

Center Trail

Feather River

Center Trail

Oak Trail

South Trail

Lake Crandall

Laurel Road

To Hwy 99

Foot of the Levee Trail

Main Levee Road

South Trail

River Bridge and continue to Laurel Avenue. Turn right (east) onto Laurel Avenue and travel 0.9 mile, past the END sign (the last 0.1 mile is unpaved), to the trailhead parking area. *DeLorme Northern California Atlas & Gazetteer:* Page 86 B1. GPS: N38 55.852 / W121 35.441

The Hike

Bobelaine Audubon Sanctuary protects a long, narrow strip of riparian habitat and oak woodland on the western banks of the Feather River. About 2.5 miles in length, a third of a mile wide, and totaling 430 acres, the ecological preserve is relatively tiny. But with frontage on the river and a wildlife population of amazing variety, it packs a scenic wallop.

Since this is an Audubon Society site located on the Pacific Flyway, you would expect to encounter a huge population of both resident and migratory birds. You won't be disappointed. But the wilderness feel of the place is unexpected. The Feather River is broad and unfettered here, weaving through sandbars and deposits of river rock and skimmed by blinding-white great egrets and clusters of diving ducks. The maples sport leaves of prehistoric size, large enough that you could wear one as a mask, completely hiding your face. Fields of sinuous tule crowd sections of the route and erupt from the trailbeds themselves, a bounty that would have kept local Indians well stocked in materials for basket weaving.

You'll share the trail with birders carrying binoculars and scopes. Whether you're an enthusiast or not, you'll be hard pressed not to be charmed and entertained by the kinglets, purple finches, and California towhees that jitter-bug through the brush; the green herons that hunker on the riverbanks and on bare tree limbs; and the hawks that swing and dance overhead. Deer and squirrels scurry through the scrub, and on hot days lizards bask on the trails.

Some but not all trail intersections are marked with signs. The lack of signage, coupled with intertwining social trails (birders are much like anglers, cutting paths through the brush to reach the best areas for sighting specific species), makes route-finding a bit of a challenge. Maps may or may not be available at the trailhead, but the information board has a map showing the sanctuary boundaries and trail system. Keep the river to the east and stay on the clear, mowed tracks—you may stray from your planned route, but you won't get lost.

The tour described here describes a loop circling counterclockwise around the sanctuary, incorporating sections of the Oak, Grasslands, North, and Center Trails.

Miles and Directions

0.0 Start by passing through the gate and onto the levee, heading right (south). The levee offers views down onto an orchard on the right (west) and the undeveloped sanctuary— a tangle of wild grapes, figs, willow, and oaks—on the left (west). A parallel trail runs along the foot of the levee; slide down onto this where the grassy face of the levee allows.

0.4 Reach the junction with a trail that drops off the levee and a singletrack trail that breaks left (east) into the preserve proper. Go left (east), around a gate, then right (south) on a singletrack trail. Signs prohibit horses, hunting, and fishing in the preserve.

0.5 At the unmarked trail intersection go left (east). This is the South Trail. Ignore side trails that wander into the brush, passing through a gully and a meadow.

0.9 Reach the signed trail intersection with the Oak Trail. Go left (north) on the Oak Trail.

1.4 Arrive at the unsigned trail intersection of the Oak Trail and the Center Trail. Stay straight (north) on the Center Trail.

1.6 At the unmarked trail junction, go right (east) on the Center Trail. The bigleaf maples along this section sport preternaturally large leaves. A broad meadow opens to the right (east).

1.9 Take the side trail that branches right (east) to the riverside. The trail stretches across a meadow to a bluff overlooking the river, which in late season is broad, curdled with current, and lovely. When you have taken in the views, retrace your steps back to the main trail and turn right (north).

2.2 Meet the signed Grassland Trail. Go right (northeast) on the Grassland Trail; a narrow track passes through fields of tule.

2.7 The Grassland Trail curves west away from the river through encroaching coyote bush.

2.9 Reach the unmarked trail junction with the North Trail. Go left (south) on the first trail (the second trail is in a large clearing and leads to the Foot of the Levee Trail).

3.6 Arrive at the junction with the Otter Trail. Go right (southwest) on the singletrack Otter Trail.

4.0 Arrive at the signed junction of the Otter Trail and the Center Trail. Go right (south) on the wide Center Trail.

4.2 At the trail intersection stay right (west) on the unsigned Center Trail. The levee rises ahead.

4.3 Pass the gate and climb onto the levee. Turn left (south), heading back toward the trailhead. A parallel trail runs along the foot of the levee, but the high road offers great views across farmlands on the right (west) and the placid Lake Crandall on the left (east).

4.6 Drop off the levee to the trailhead and parking area.

2 Codfish Falls (Auburn State Recreation Area)

The trail to Codfish Falls has the flavor of an alpine adventure, skimming through a secluded portion of the North Fork American River canyon to a pretty, tucked-away cascade.

Distance: 3.2 miles out and back
Approximate hiking time: 2 hours
Difficulty: Moderate due to length and uneven trail surface
Trail surface: Dirt singletrack
Best season: Spring and fall. The summer sun may be blistering (though you can cool off in the river), and winter rain and snow may render the trail inhospitable.
Other trail users: Mountain bikers (but not many)
Canine compatibility: Leashed dogs permitted
Fees and permits: No fees or permits required
Schedule: Open 6:00 a.m. to 9:00 p.m. daily in summer; 7:00 a.m. to 7:00 p.m. daily in winter
Maps: USGS Colfax and Greenwood; Auburn State Recreation

Area brochure available at the recreation headquarters on Highway 49 and at www.parks.ca.gov
Trail contact: Auburn State Recreation Area, 501 El Dorado Street, Auburn 95603-4949; (530) 885-4527; www.park.ca .gov; e-mail: asra@parks.ca.gov
Special considerations: The trailhead is remote, reached via a steep, winding country road. The final 2.4 miles of the road are unpaved, and a high-clearance car is recommended.

This is rattlesnake and mountain lion country. Proceed with caution, and use the proper safety precautions should you encounter either creature on the trail.
Additional information: Trailhead amenities include roadside parking for about ten cars. There are no restrooms. Bring drinking water.

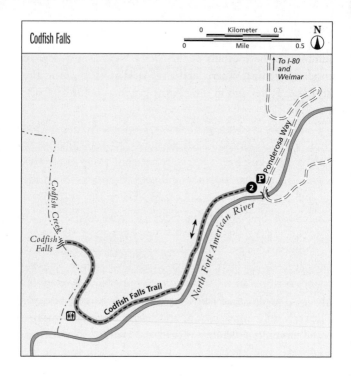

Codfish Falls

Kilometer 0.5

Mile 0.5

N

Codfish Creek

Codfish Falls

Codfish Falls Trail

North Fork American River

To I-80 and Weimar

Ponderosa Way

P 2

Finding the trailhead: Follow Interstate 80 east of Sacramento to the hamlet of Weimar in the Sierra foothills (about 11 miles east of Auburn). Take the Weimar Cross Road exit and turn right (west, then southwest) onto Ponderosa Way. Follow Ponderosa to a gate at the end of the pavement at 3.2 miles, then down the steep, rutted dirt road into the canyon for another 2.4 miles to the bridge over the North Fork American River (5.6 miles total). Park along the wide stretch of road just northeast of the bridge. The trail is beyond the metal guardrails at the bridge's north abutment. *DeLorme Northern California Atlas & Gazetteer:* Pages 79 D7 and 87 A6. GPS: N39 00.028 / W120 56.391

The Hike

Summer in the foothills of the Sierra Nevada is a time of unrelenting sun. Where better to beat it than along the American River and in the narrow canyon cooled by Codfish Falls.

The trail leading to these secluded falls follows the North Fork American River, skirting cool pools that invite side trips to sandbars and rocky beaches along the riverbank. The falls flow down a jumble of dark rocks in a shady enclave just north of the river valley. They run year-round and water a pocket of verdant mosses, oaks, and grasses in an otherwise parched environment.

Ponderosa Way, which dives into the American River canyon from Weimar, offers a huge hint at how out-of-bounds this stretch of trail in the Auburn State Recreation Area is. The dirt road falls steeply into the gorge, requiring a driver's full concentration, and heightening anticipation, as the terrain grows more rugged and remote. The narrow singletrack trail departs from the north abutment of the sturdy but rustic metal-trussed Ponderosa Way Bridge, tracing the river's course for about a mile before curving north into the Codfish Creek canyon.

River views dominate the dirt track. The route is sometimes rocky and sometimes exposed but always easy to negotiate. Markers along the trail are keyed to an interpretive guide that may be stocked in the mailbox at the trail sign 0.25 mile downstream from the bridge . . . and maybe not. No matter: The scenery speaks for itself. Perched on the interface of oak woodlands dominating lower elevations and evergreen forests that flourish higher up, the mixed forest includes oaks and red-barked mountain manzanita, the occasional madrone, and ponderosa pines. Pause at the golden-barked pines to sniff their vanilla scent—hugging a tree has never smelled so sweet.

Though the river is placid and clear in late season, it swells with snowmelt in spring and early summer. Wait for the flow to mellow before you dip your toes into the water. Fishing and rafting are also popular here.

Miles and Directions

0.0 Start on the north side of the Ponderosa Way Bridge, climbing over the guardrail onto the singletrack trail. A beach spreads below the trail, offering access to the cooling waters of the North Fork American River.

0.2 Pass a Codfish Falls/Discovery Trail sign and a mailbox that may hold interpretive guides.

0.4 Flat sheets of shale pave a patch of trail. Pass Markers 3 and 4.

0.6 Pass Marker 6; the trail here is about 30 feet above the river, separated from the water by a relatively steep, rocky slope.

0.8 The trail narrows in a gully showing signs of erosion.

1.0 A narrow social trail breaks left (southeast) to the river. Stay straight on the obvious Codfish Falls Trail.

1.1 The trail curls northwest, away from the river.

1.2 Pass a little outhouse. The trail splits just beyond, with a couple of social tracks leading left (southeast) back toward the river. Stay right (northwest), heading up the side canyon toward the falls.

1.4 Cross a seasonal stream, dry in the late season. The trail gently climbs through the mixed evergreen forest.

1.6 Reach Codfish Falls and the final interpretive marker (14). Enjoy the falls and then return as you came.

3.2 Arrive back at the trailhead.

3 Mountain Quarry Railroad Trail (Auburn State Recreation Area)

The abandoned bed of the Mountain Quarry Railroad rolls across the historic No Hands Bridge and then follows the American River downstream through a lovely stretch of canyon.

Distance: 4.2 miles out and back

Approximate hiking time: 2 hours

Difficulty: Moderate due to the trail's length

Trail surface: Dirt and ballast on a former railroad bed

Best season: Spring and fall. Summer may be very hot, but you can cool off in the water. Winter rains or snow may render the track muddy, but it generally dries out within a couple of days.

Other trail users: Trail runners. Mountains bikers are not permitted on the trail, but tracks in the dirt indicate they poach the route.

Canine compatibility: Leashed dogs permitted

Fees and permits: No fees or permits required

Schedule: Open 6:00 a.m. to 9:00 p.m. daily in summer; 7:00 a.m. to 7:00 p.m. daily in winter

Maps: USGS Auburn; Auburn State Recreation Area brochure available at the recreation headquarters on Highway 49 and at www.parks.ca.gov

Trail contact: Auburn State Recreation Area, 501 El Dorado Street, Auburn 95603-4949; (530) 885-4527; www.park.ca .gov; e-mail: asra@parks.ca.gov

Special considerations: This is rattlesnake and mountain lion country. Proceed with caution, and use the proper safety precautions should you encounter either creature on the trail. Other potential hazards include poison oak, which causes skin irritation, and ticks, which may carry Lyme disease. These can be avoided by staying on the trail.

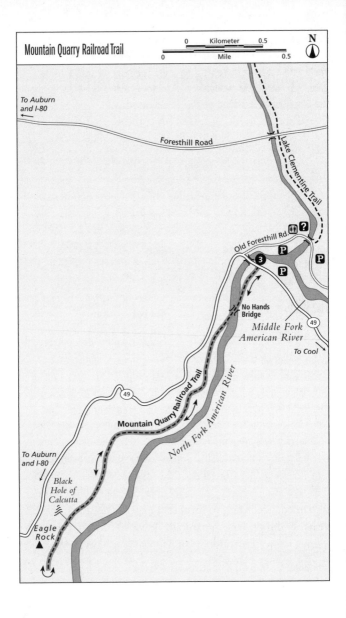

Kilometer
0
0.5

Mile
0
0.5

N

To Auburn
and I-80

Foresthill Road

Lake Clementine Trail

Old Foresthill Rd.

P

?

3

P

P

No Hands
Bridge

Middle Fork
American River

49

To Cool

Mountain Quarry Railroad Trail

North Fork American River

49

To Auburn
and I-80

Black
Hole of
Calcutta

Eagle
Rock

Additional information: Trailhead amenities are minimal. You'll find a trash can behind the gate. Restrooms are available at the Stagecoach trailhead on the west side of the Old Foresthill Bridge, about 0.5 mile north of the Highway 49 trailhead. No water is available; bring all that you need.

Finding the trailhead: From Interstate 80 head east to the Highway 49 exit in Auburn. Take Highway 49 south through Auburn, following the signs for 0.5 mile through the downtown area to where the highway plunges down into the American River canyon. Highway 49 meets Old Foresthill Road at the base of the hill at 2.5 miles. Turn right (southeast), cross the bridge, and park alongside the road. The trailhead (marked 150) is at the gate on the southeast side of the bridge. *DeLorme Northern California Atlas & Gazetteer:* Page 87 6A. GPS: N38 54.894 / W121 2.404

The Hike

Abundant riches typical of California's Mother Lode surround this easy route—not riches that can be mined from mountainsides or sifted from river bottoms, mind you, but the wealth of a wildland journey through the steep-walled American River canyon.

The Mountain Quarry Railroad Trail lies on the bed of a historic rail line that once linked a limestone quarry on the Middle Fork American River with the town of Auburn and Southern Pacific tracks that continued to Sacramento. The rail trail includes passage over the No Hands Bridge, so named, according to local trail experts, because for many years it didn't have guardrails (now it does). Once the longest concrete bridge of its kind in the world, the scenic bridge survived the collapse of the Hell Hole Dam in 1964, as well as subsequent floods, and now provides hikers with a tangible encounter with history.

Enjoyably straightforward, the trail deviates from the original rail line only where trestles have been removed. Their concrete abutments, overgrown with oak scrub and inscribed with the dates they were poured—1915, 1921—overlook drops through gullies. Unable to negotiate the steep curves of the terrain, trestles straightened the line. Hikers have no such luck, but swinging through folds in the canyon wall poses no hardship to those on foot.

Along the track you'll encounter numerous signs that you follow a rail line, including sections where cut-and-fill construction techniques have resulted in grass-covered berms that cradle the trail. Railroads, even in the mountains, had to follow gentle grades, and the Mountain Quarries line was no exception. You'll encounter only one steep set of pitches along the route, where the trail dips into a gully washed by a small waterfall dubbed the "Black Hole of Calcutta." The year-round cascade offers a dark, cooling respite along the track.

The rest of the route is flat, sunny, and pleasant, offering great views down to the river and across to the wooded slopes on the far side. The exposed section of trail at the base of Eagle Rock—a steep, flaking monolith with debris spilling downslope—is particularly striking. Side trails lead both uphill and down to riverside, but stay straight and flat and you'll never lose your way.

If there's a downside to this route, it's only that road noise from nearby Highway 49 echoes in the canyon. The scenic and historic attributes of the route mitigate this potential distraction.

The Mountain Quarry Railroad Trail is a portion of the

Western States Pioneer Express Recreation Trail, 100 miles long and the venue for endurance races for runners and equestrians. For more information call the Western States Trail Foundation at (530) 823-7282.

Miles and Directions

0.0 Start at the gate on the southeast side of the bridge.

0.2 Pass the junction with the steep Pointed Rocks Trail (a trail sign indicates this leads to Cool) on the left (south). Go right (west) across the No Hands Bridge.

0.3 Reach Marker 3 on the west side of the No Hands Bridge and continue on the obvious rail trail. An interpretive sign at the end of the bridge offers information about its historic significance.

0.6 Pass a Western States Pioneer Express Recreation Trail sign and a pair of side trails. Remain on the obvious rail trail.

0.8 Reach the first trestle abutment. The trail departs from the railroad grade, narrows to singletrack, and scoops through a gully.

1.0 Pass a trestle foundation dated 1915.

1.1 Reach the only steep drop and climb of the route, through the "Black Hole of Calcutta." Once back on the railroad grade, pass another marker for the Western States Pioneer Express Recreation Trail.

1.3 Pass another trestle abutment.

1.4 At the unmarked trail intersection, stay left (straight/west) on the obvious railroad grade.

1.7 Skirt the giant, flaking rock face of Eagle Rock.

2.1 Pass a mile marker and another Western States Pioneer Express Recreation Trail marker at the end of the railroad grade. This is the turnaround point. Retrace your steps to the trailhead.

4.2 Arrive back at the trailhead.

Option: You can link the first 0.5 mile of this trail with the first 0.5 mile of the Lake Clementine Trail in an interpretive loop. Pick up a copy of *American River Canyon Hikes,* available at local retailers or online at www.canyonkeepers .org, and follow the directions for the Confluence Interpretive Trail, which is keyed to numbered posts along both stretches of trail. A short stretch of roadside hiking separates the Mountain Quarry Railroad Trail from the Lake Clementine trailhead. Follow Highway 49 back across the bridge and then follow Old Foresthill Road right (north), across the Old Foresthill Road Bridge, to the Lake Clementine trailhead.

4 Lake Clementine Trail (Auburn State Recreation Area)

This scenic trail traces the North Fork American River, passes under the scenic Foresthill Bridge, offers access to a cool swimming hole, and culminates at an overlook of Lake Clementine's waterfall spillway.

Distance: 4.6 miles out and back

Approximate hiking time: 2.5 hours

Difficulty: Moderate due to trail length

Trail surface: Dirt roadway, short stretches of paved road, and dirt singletrack

Best season: Spring and fall

Other trail users: Mountain bikers, equestrians, trail runners

Canine compatibility: Leashed dogs permitted

Fees and permits: No fees or permits required

Schedule: Open 6:00 a.m. to 9:00 p.m. daily in summer; 7:00 a.m. to 7:00 p.m. daily in winter

Maps: USGS Auburn; Auburn State Recreation Area brochure available at the recreation headquarters on Highway 49 and at www.parks.ca.gov

Trail contact: Auburn State Recreation Area, 501 El Dorado Street, Auburn 95603-4949; (530) 885-4527; www.park.ca .gov; e-mail: asra@parks.ca.gov

Special considerations: The recreation area is home to mountain lions and rattlesnakes. Use proper safety precautions should you encounter either creature on the trail. Other potential hazards include poison oak, which causes skin irritation, and ticks, which may carry Lyme disease. These can be avoided by staying on the trail.

Additional information: There are no amenities at the trailhead proper. However, there are restrooms, information boards, and additional parking at the Stagecoach trailhead on the west side of the Old Foresthill Road Bridge.

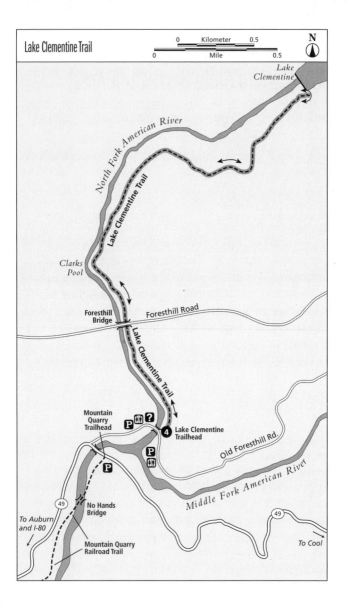

Lake Clementine Trail

N

0   Kilometer   0.5
0   Mile   0.5

Lake Clementine

North Fork American River

Lake Clementine Trail

Clarks Pool

Foresthill Road

Foresthill Bridge

Lake Clementine Trail

Mountain Quarry Trailhead

4 Lake Clementine Trailhead

Old Foresthill Rd.

Middle Fork American River

49

No Hands Bridge

To Auburn and I-80

Mountain Quarry Railroad Trail

To Cool

49

Finding the trailhead: From Interstate 80 in Auburn, take the Highway 49/Placerville exit. Follow Highway 49 south through downtown Auburn (signs point the way) for about 0.5 mile to where the highway dives into the American River canyon. Proceed another 2.5 miles to the floor of the canyon and the junction of Highway 49 and Old Foresthill Road. Continue for about 0.5 mile on Old Foresthill Road to the trailhead on the left, on the west side of the Old Foresthill Road Bridge. Parking is alongside the roadway just beyond the bridge. The trail begins behind the gate (#139, signed for Lake Clementine). *DeLorme Northern California Atlas & Gazetteer:* Page 87 6A. GPS: N38 54.978 / W121 2.129

The Hike

The confluence of the north and middle forks of the American River, in the bottom of a steep, spectacular canyon northeast of Sacramento, draws thousands of visitors to the Auburn State Recreation Area each year. The river valleys—and the historic sites within them—have long been slated for submersion beneath a huge and controversial reservoir. But the Auburn Dam has been besieged by seismic, environmental, and economic concerns since construction began in the mid-1960s, and the process was brought to an apparently permanent halt in late 2008, when water rights held by the U.S. Bureau of Reclamation were revoked. If completed, the dam would have drowned the river behind a 690-foot wall, and the popular trails that explore the forks would have drowned along with it. Now (hopefully) they can be enjoyed in perpetuity.

The trail to Lake Clementine showcases the lovely natural setting of the canyon, but man-made structures also draw the eye. The green lattice arches and massive concrete support columns of the Foresthill Bridge frame the trail's outset, the boom and clank of cars passing overhead echoing into the canyon. At trail's end, a sheet of water spills over the North Fork Dam, with Lake Clementine pooling behind. Markers along the first 0.5 mile of the route (which is part of the Confluence Interpretive Loop) are keyed to a guide published by the Auburn State Recreation Area Canyon Keepers and highlight historic sites along the trail.

Foresthill Bridge, reportedly the tallest in California, was built to span the reservoir that never materialized. Below, the wide dirt road to Lake Clementine follows the river's curves, intercepted by anglers' trails that drop to the banks. The foundations of lesser bridges, some historic, jut from forested hillsides scarred by minor slides and small fires. Islands and rocky shoals in the midst of the river harbor stands of willow that blush yellow in fall.

A little less than a mile upstream from the confluence, the north fork widens and deepens into Clarks Pool, a popular swimming spot formed by an "underwater dam" built by placer miners more than one hundred years ago, according to the Canyon Keepers. The trail begins an easy, steady climb beyond the hole, eventually reaching the paved Lake Clementine Road. A short trek down the pavement and along a dirt singletrack trail leads to an up-close and personal view of the waterfall spillway of Lake Clementine. This is the prefect spot to snack, rest, and watch the boats ply the smooth waters of a reservoir that actually came to be.

Miles and Directions

0.0 Start behind Gate 139, signed for Lake Clementine.

0.1 Stay left (riverside) at the unmarked trail fork.

0.2 Pass Marker 7 at the concrete bridge abutment.

0.5	The trail narrows to singletrack as it passes beneath the massive support tower of the Foresthill Bridge.
0.8	Reach the southernmost edge of Clarks Pool. Social trails drop left to riverside for the length of the pond-smooth pool. (**Option:** This is a good turnaround point for families and those seeking a shorter hike.)
1.0	The abutment for a historic (now defunct) covered bridge juts from the opposite bank. The trail begins to climb.
1.2	Pass a social trail leading down to the riverside. The trail continues to climb through oaks and scrub, with limited views opening of the North Fork Dam and Lake Clementine.
1.8	Arrive at the end of the dirt road/trail at a gate. Go left (north, then northeast) on the paved roadway.
2.2	A singletrack path leads left (north) toward the dam over-look.
2.3	Reach the overlook. Take in the views before retracing your steps to the trailhead.
4.6	Arrive back at the trailhead and Old Foresthill Road Bridge.

Option: You can link the first 0.5 mile of this trail, from the trailhead to Clarks Pool, with the first 0.5 mile of the Mountain Quarry Railroad Trail in an interpretive loop. Pick up a copy of *American River Canyon Hikes,* available at local retailers or online at www.canyonkeepers.org, and follow the directions for the Confluence Interpretive Trail, which is keyed to numbered posts along both stretches of trail.

5 East Ridge–Long Valley Trail Loop (Cronan Ranch Regional Trails Park)

Winding ranch roads sweep through meadows thick with wildflowers in spring and then drop to beaches along a rumbling stretch of the South Fork American River.

Distance: 4.4-mile loop

Approximate hiking time: 2.5 hours

Difficulty: More challenging due to distance and steep pitches on the descent

Trail surface: Dirt ranch roads

Best season: Spring for wildflowers; fall for cool weather

Other trail users: Equestrians, mountain bikers, trail runners

Canine compatibility: Leashed dogs permitted. However, dogs commonly run off-leash. If you allow your dog to run off-leash, keep your pet under voice control to avoid conflicts with equestrians.

Fees and permits: No fees or permits required

Schedule: Open from sunrise to sunset daily

Maps: USGS Coloma; trail map and brochure available at www.ca.blm.gov/folsom

Trail contact: Bureau of Land Management, Folsom Field Office, 63 Natoma Street, Folsom 95630; (916) 985-4474; www.ca.blm.gov/folsom; www.blm.gov/ca/st/en/fo/folsom/cronan.html

Special considerations: This is rattlesnake and mountain lion country. Proceed with caution, and use the proper safety precautions should you encounter either creature on the trail. If you permit your dog to run off-leash, your pet risks a rattlesnake bite as well.

Additional information: Trailhead amenities include restrooms, trash cans, ample parking for cars and horse trailers, and an information board with maps.

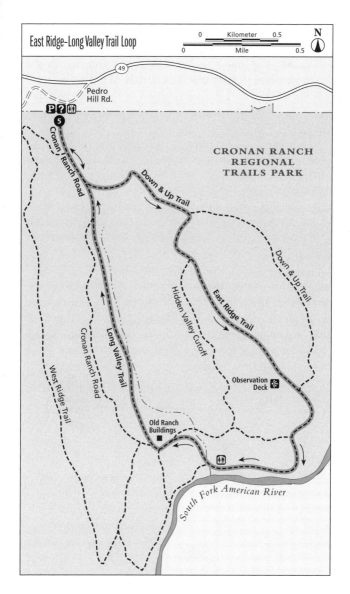

East Ridge-Long Valley Trail Loop

Kilometer

Mile

N

Pedro
Hill Rd.

49

P ? ♿
5

Cronan Ranch Road

CRONAN RANCH
REGIONAL
TRAILS PARK

Down & Up Trail

Down & Up Trail

East Ridge Trail

Hidden Valley Cutoff

Long Valley Trail

Cronan Ranch Road

West Ridge Trail

Observation
Deck ♨

Old Ranch
Buildings

♿

South Fork American River

Finding the trailhead: From Interstate 80 in Auburn, take the Highway 49/Placerville exit and head south toward Placerville. Follow Highway 49 for 11.5 miles, through Auburn into the American River canyon and then up through the hamlets of Cool and Pilot Hill, to Pedro Hill Road on the right (west). Follow Pedro Hill Road south for 0.1 mile to the signed parking area on the left (south) side of the road.

Alternatively, you can take U.S. Highway 50 east out of Sacramento to the junction with Highway 49 in Placerville. Turn left (north) onto Highway 49 and follow it for 14.2 miles through Marshall Gold Discovery State Historic Park to Pedro Hill Road on the left (west). *DeLorme Northern California Atlas & Gazetteer:* Page 87 B6. GPS: N38 48.242 / W120 53.687

The Hike

On cool autumn afternoons, with the sun low in the sky, the foothills of Cronan Ranch Regional Trails Park take on smoky hues, darker where the forests grow thick on north slopes and lighter where the sun catches the golden annual grasses. The scene is arresting.

A wonderful network of trails laces through Cronan Ranch, spreading equestrians, mountain bikers, and hikers along ridges and tucking them into long valleys. All roads lead eventually to the South Fork American River, which constitutes portions of the property's southern and eastern boundaries. The river, even when the flow is low, rumbles swiftly over its bed, more inviting to rafters and anglers than to swimmers and waders. Still, spread a picnic on a blanket on the rocky shore, with the relentless music of the water rushing by, and you'll enjoy a restful and invigorating break.

The grasses coating the hills are nonnative annuals, inadvertently brought to California by Spanish conquistadors and missionaries in the mid-1700s. They grow green in the rainy season and burn gold in summer, painted with native wildflowers—lupines, poppies, yarrow, asters, fiddlenecks, and Indian paintbrush—in season. The grasses have long supported grazing animals, from the deer and elk hunted by native Californians who summered in the foothills to the cattle that the Cronan family raised after purchasing the property from the Central Pacific Railroad. A cluster of ramshackle ranch buildings at the junction of the Long Valley Trail and Cronan Ranch Road hearken back to what must have been a lonely but lovely occupation for the Cronans and the families that followed.

Today the property is part of a plan to create a South Fork American River trail corridor that would stretch from Greenwood Creek to Salmon Falls, according to BLM park literature. Equestrians, mountain bikers, and hikers easily share the trails already in place, as do the paragliders who climb to high launching points and then ride the thermals with the hawks and vultures.

This route descends into the river canyon via the Down and Up and East Ridge Trails, easy-to-follow ranch roads that descend steeply in sections. You'll follow the river downstream past rocky bars and picnic sites and then climb back to the trailhead along the more gently inclined Long Valley Trail. You can do the loop in the opposite direction, but the climb up the East Ridge Trail will punish you.

Miles and Directions

0.0   Start on the Cronan Ranch Road, heading uphill through the grassland.

0.1   At the junction with the West Ridge Trail, stay straight (south) on Cronan Ranch Road.

0.2 Arrive at an information board and the junction with the Down and Up Trail. Go left (east) on the Down and Up Trail, also a former ranch road.

0.6 Pass the wind sock used by paragliders, who launch off the hilltop to the left (north) of the trail.

0.8 At the intersection of the Down and Up and East Ridge Trails, go right (southwest) on the East Ridge Trail. Views open down toward the river valley.

1.0 Pass the junction with the Hidden Valley Cutoff, staying left (south) on the East Ridge Trail. The route is open, with only scattered shade, and saturated in views of the cushioning hills and glinting river.

1.5 A side trail leads to a rickety observation platform, which sported rotting boards and missing railings in late 2008. The vistas are great whether you take them in from the platform or not. The trail steepens as you continue.

1.8 Arrive at the lower junction of the Down and Up and East Ridge Trails. Go right (southwest) on the Down and Up Trail, passing through a fenceline. The forested north slope of the river canyon hosts dirt tracks used by off-road vehicles, and the whine of motorcycle engines sometimes rips through the quiet. No motorized vehicles are allowed in the regional park.

2.1 At the next junction, marked by a trail sign bearing only an arrow, stay left (south/downhill) into the riverside bottomlands.

2.3 Ignore side trails that lead left as you reach the river. Continue right (downriver/west) until you find the perfect spot to soak your feet, eat your lunch, and let the dog go for a swim. The riverfront is dotted with portable toilets, but no potable water is available.

2.6 Pass the first road/trail that climbs right (north/uphill) out of the river valley. The trail is unsigned. Stay straight (west) on the riverside track.

2.7 Pass a restroom with an unsigned trail leading uphill behind it. Cross a seasonal stream and then take the second trail leading uphill (north). This is Cronan Ranch Road.

2.9 Climb past a signed intersection with the Down and Up Trail. Stay left (up/west) on Cronan Ranch Road.

3.1 Bear right on the ranch road through a cluster of old ranch buildings to a three-way trail intersection. An unsigned trail departs to the left (south). Cronan Ranch Road is the middle track, and the Long Valley Trail departs to the right (north). You can follow either Cronan Ranch Road or Long Valley to the trailhead. The Long Valley Trail is described here, traveling up the valley floor alongside a seasonal stream that, even when dry, nourishes a green stroke of reeds, willow, and bay.

3.7 Cross a culvert that channels an intermittent stream.

4.0 The Long Valley Trail ends on Cronan Ranch Road. Turn right (north) onto Cronan Ranch Road.

4.2 Reach the end of the loop at the junction with the Down and Up Trail. From here retrace your steps to the trailhead.

4.4 Arrive back at the trailhead and parking area.

6 Dave Moore Nature Trail

This sweet little route meanders through oak woodlands down to a rocky beach on the American River, offering the wheelchair-bound, the stroller-bound, and the able-bodied easy access to a backcountry experience.

Distance: 1.1-mile loop
Approximate hiking time: 1 hour
Difficulty: Easy
Trail surface: Wheelchair-accessible decomposed granite path, dirt singletrack
Best season: Spring through fall
Other trail users: None
Canine compatibility: Leashed dogs permitted
Fees and permits: No fees or permits required
Schedule: Open 8:00 a.m. to sunset daily
Maps: USGS Coloma
Trail contact: Bureau of Land Management, Folsom Field Office, 63 Natoma Street, Folsom 95630; (916) 985-4474; www

.blm.gov/ca/st/en/fo/folsom/dmna.html
Special considerations: Remain on the trail to avoid contact with poison oak. This is rattlesnake and mountain lion country. Should you encounter a snake or a cat on the trail, follow the advice offered in the introduction to this guide.
Additional information: Trailhead amenities include lots of parking in a gravel lot, a vault toilet, and picnic tables. Bring drinking water. The first 0.5 mile of the trail is wheelchair and stroller accessible. The South Fork American River is a delightful place to wade in the hot months of summer and fall.

Finding the trailhead: From Interstate 80 in Auburn, take the Highway 49/Placerville exit and head south. Follow Highway 49 for about 15.7 miles through Auburn, down into the American River canyon, and then up through the hamlets of Cool and Pilot Hill to the

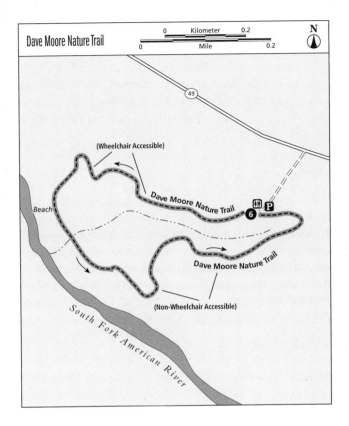

nature area's entrance on the right (west). The entry is well signed and bordered by large cobblestone walls. Follow the dirt access road west for 0.1 mile to the parking area.

Alternatively, you can take U.S. Highway 50 east out of Sacramento to the junction with Highway 49 in Placerville. Turn left (north) onto Highway 49 and follow it for about 10 miles through Marshall Gold Discovery State Historic Park to the trailhead access road on the left (west). *DeLorme Northern California Atlas & Gazetteer:* Page 87 B7. GPS: N38 48.923 / W120 55.246

The Hike

Following the sweeping curves of the rock-lined Dave Moore Nature Trail is reminiscent of walking a labyrinth. The first 0.5 mile curls thoughtfully through the oak woodlands, offering travelers ample chance to contemplate what draws them outdoors—how the sun filters through a forest canopy, the unique shapes of rocks and boulders, how fleeting glimpses of a nearby river quicken the senses.

Walking or rolling from the trailhead to the rocky banks of the South Fork American River is an absolute pleasure. Surfaced in decomposed granite, the route spans seasonal streams via sturdy bridges and handles grades via gentle switchbacks that sweep past, among other things, a huge old madrone ring, a boulder that pops from the forest floor like a button mushroom, and the handiwork of Chinese laborers who, during the gold rush, carved ditches and built rock walls to aid miners in their quest to recover precious nuggets.

The trail is dedicated to the memory of a Bureau of Land Management conservation ranger who was stricken with multiple sclerosis. The wheelchair- and stroller-accessible stretch ends on a little riverside beach. The South Fork American River is shallow here in summer and fall, skipping over a rocky bed. Willows and oaks shade the spot, which is perfect for picnicking and wading.

The second half of the loop is decidedly not wheelchair accessible, growing narrow and rocky as it continues along the riverfront and then bending eastward through the woodlands back to the trailhead. You'll find seclusion here, as many visitors return as they came, on the wheelchair-accessible path.

Miles and Directions

0.0 Start at the trailhead on the north side of the parking area, behind the restroom.

0.1 At the trail fork stay left on the rock-lined path toward a picnic table, then switchback down to where the paths merge at the bridge.

0.2 Cross another bridge amid blackberry brambles, then pass the button mushroom rock and a picnic table on the left. The path narrows through a gully where the trail is softened by pine needles, switchbacks down to and across another bridge, and rambles alongside a rock wall.

0.4 Switchback around two bridges that lead to the rocky little beach on the South Fork American River. The wheelchair-accessible portion of the trail ends here. Picnic and play, then return to the trail and turn right (southeast). (**Option:** Retrace your steps to the trailhead if you are unable to negotiate the non-wheelchair-accessible portion.)

0.5 A bridge spans a seasonal stream. Wildflowers, willows, and reeds encroach on the path, which narrows and becomes rocky as it skirts trees and rock outcrops. Signs indicate this is a habitat restoration area.

0.7 Swing left (north), away from the river and into a cut in the bank. A split log bridge spans a seasonal stream. Stay on the maintained trail along the streambed, avoiding social paths that are blocked by water bars.

0.9 Climb into a parklike grove of oaks, which line the trail like an avenue, and then circle northwest toward the parking lot, passing another restoration sign.

1.1 Cross a bridge over a seasonal stream. Pass a trail that leads right (east) to a picnic spot and arrive back at the trailhead parking area.

7 Monroe Ridge–Marshall Monument Trail Loop (Marshall Gold Discovery State Historic Park)

Climb through oak woodlands to viewpoints above the snaking South Fork American River. Then tour a historic gold rush town, including the site where the precious metal was discovered in 1848.

Distance: 3.8-mile loop

Approximate hiking time: 2 hours

Difficulty: More challenging due to trail length and generous changes in elevation

Trail surface: Dirt singletrack, some paved roadways and rustic sidewalks, gravel paths

Best season: Year-round, though winter storms and cold may render the trail inhospitable

Other trail users: None

Canine compatibility: Dogs not permitted

Fees and permits: $5 day-use fee, paid at the visitor center

Schedule: Open 8:00 a.m. to sunset daily

Maps: USGS Coloma; state historic park map available at the visitor center/museum and at

www.parks.ca.gov

Trail contact: California State Parks, P.O. Box 942896, Sacramento 94296; (800) 777-0369; www.parks.ca.gov; park address: P.O. Box 265, Coloma 95613; (530) 622-3470

Special considerations: The trail ventures into mountain lion and rattlesnake country. Should you encounter either a snake or a cat on the trail, follow the advice offered in the introduction to this guide.

Additional information: You'll find paved parking, restrooms, water, and picnic facilities at the North Beach trailhead. There is no water along the trail, but there is water at the trailhead and a drinking fountain at the Marshall Monument site.

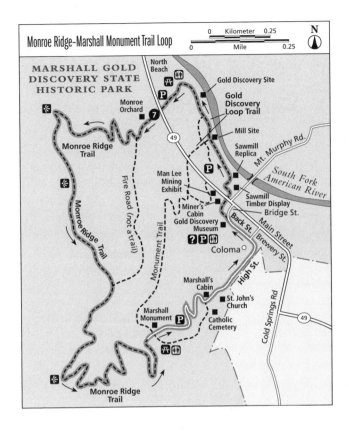

Restrooms, information, picnic sites, a museum, and a gift shop are available at the visitor center. The museum houses dioramas describing native tribes that lived in the area; natural history and gold rush history; reproductions of gold nuggets; collections of artifacts from gold rush days, including old bottles, assay instruments, and household items; and an old stagecoach. April through Labor Day weekend the museum is open Tuesday through Sunday from 10:00 a.m. to 4:30 p.m. After Labor Day through March the hours are 10:00 a.m. to 3:00 p.m.

The museum is closed Monday from July 1 to February 28. The park is closed on Thanksgiving, Christmas, and New Year's Day.

The museum's address is 310 Back Street, Coloma 95613; the number is (530) 622-3470.

Finding the trailhead: Head west from Sacramento on U.S. Highway 50 to Placerville and the junction with Highway 49. Turn left (north) onto Highway 49 and follow the scenic road for 9 miles through the town of Coloma and past the visitor center to the North Beach picnic area and parking area on the right (east). Park in the southernmost part of the parking area; the trailhead is across Highway 49 from the lot, at a break in the split-rail fence near the old mining cabin. *DeLorme Northern California Atlas & Gazetteer:* Page 87 B7. GPS: N38 48.245 / W120 53.698

The Hike

Yes, you can still pan for gold along the South Fork American River. But that's not the only kind of wealth that can be gleaned from these hills. The canyon walls hovering over Sutter's Mill offer spectacular views up and down the river valley, and the state park that commemorates the discovery of gold is a treasure chest of historic sites and information.

The story is familiar to most Californians, but I'll recap just in case: In 1848 James Marshall, who ran a Coloma lumber mill in partnership with John Sutter, was checking the mill's tailrace and discovered gold flakes in the detritus that had backed up there. One of the largest gold rushes in history followed, with thousands of fortune seekers racing to the Sierra from all over the world. The rush itself was short-lived, but in its aftermath California, acquired from Mexico in the same year Marshall made his discovery, became America's "Golden State."

Coloma and the state park are pretty much one and the same. Some old miners' cabins, including that of James Marshall, are preserved intact; other historic homes have been transformed into bed-and-breakfasts and private residences. Storefronts that date back to the gold rush now house historic exhibits, restaurants, and gift shops. Along the Gold Discovery Loop Trail, which meanders down by the river, a reproduction of Sutter's Mill overlooks picnic grounds, and a striking river-rock monument marks the original mill site. A bronze statue of Marshall stands on a pedestal on the southwest side of the canyon, overlooking the entire scene.

This route, while saturated in history, also rises above it. It begins and ends at the Monroe homesite: The matriarch of the Monroe family was a former slave who purchased her son's freedom with money earned working for miners. The family remained in Coloma for more than a century before selling their property to the state. The trail climbs the steep canyon wall via a number of switchbacks, winding through stands of red-barked mountain manzanita, oaks, and, in its upper reaches, ponderosa pines. Road noise from Highway 49 filters up through the trees but fades as you climb.

The trail tops out on a forested ridge where picnic tables offer rest stops with expansive vistas of the river valley. More switchbacks drop though the mixed woodland back into town, landing at the Marshall Monument, where you can enjoy the same views as the ghost of the man.

The path back to the Monroe homesite meanders along peaceful country roads lined with historic buildings to the banks of the American River. Here the Gold Discovery Loop Trail explores the mill and discovery sites. Back at North Beach you can rest on the riverbank and mull the possibilities of your success as a placer miner.

Miles and Directions

0.0 Start on the Monroe Ridge Trail, climbing past a mining cabin and through the remnants of the Monroe family orchards.

0.1 Stay right (up/southwest) on the singletrack Monroe Ridge Trail, avoiding the fire road on the left.

0.2 Switchbacks lead to a staircase and bridge across a flume that was used for mining and irrigation.

0.6 Pass a twisted manzanita that reaches north to valley views at a switchback. Keep up!

0.8 A long ascending traverse attains the ridgetop, then follows its spine south to a picnic table in a stand of oaks. Spectacular views drop hundreds of feet to the river and Coloma.

1.1 Pass a side trail to a fenced-off pit on the left (south). Stay right (southwest) on the Monroe Ridge Trail.

1.2 Reach a saddle with low-slung power lines overhead.

1.5 Arrive at a second picnic bench and overlook. Enjoy a rest and then continue on the now-descending Monroe Ridge Trail. Switchbacks drop across sunny south-facing slopes that bloom with wildflowers in season. Pass a trail sign and a short path to a vista point.

2.1 More than a half dozen switchbacks lead down to a trail marker at a clearing in the woodland. A covered cistern sits uphill to the right (south). Stay left (east), heading toward the Marshall Monument.

2.2 The path meets the paved park road at a picnic area. Walk left (uphill) on the road toward the park residence, then go right (east) on the signed Marshall Monument path (also paved). Stairs lead up to the monument site, where Marshall's bronze likeness stands atop a marble-and-granite pedestal overlooking Coloma and the river valley. Take in the views, read the interpretive signs, drink the sweet water from the fountain, then descend the steps to the paved road and go left (east), following the road leading down into the historic district.

2.8 Reach Marshall's Cabin and St. John's Catholic Church and cemetery. Continue east on High Street, passing historic homes and sites as you continue.

3.0 At the corner of Back and Brewery Streets turn left (north), passing the ruins of the El Dorado County Jail.

3.1 Back Street leads to Bridge Street and the visitor center/museum. Follow the interpretive trail through the mining equipment exhibit. Cross Highway 49 and turn left (north), passing the Gold Trail Grange building to the Gold Discovery Loop Trail. (**Option:** You can wander at will in the historic district, with side streets and trails leading to a variety of sites and activities.)

3.3 Visit the Sutter's Mill replica, then follow the crushed granite riverside path left (north).

3.5 The original site of Sutter's Mill and the gold discovery site follow in quick succession—the first a huge cobblestone monument on the riverbank, the second a pond of still water where even the most skeptical visitor can't help but hope she'll spot a gold flake . . .

3.8 Continue north along the riverside path to trail's end at the North Beach picnic grounds and parking lot.

8 Beeks Bight Nature Trail (Folsom Lake State Recreation Area)

The oak woodland ecology of Folsom Lake frames this short interpretive trail along the shoreline of a relatively isolated bay.

Distance: 1.1 mile out and back (loop at low water)
Approximate hiking time: 1 hour
Difficulty: Easy
Trail surface: Dirt and gravel singletrack
Best season: Spring for wildflowers; fall and winter for cool temperatures. High summer temperatures may restrict hiking to the mornings and evenings. Wait a few days after a heavy winter rain for the trail to dry out.
Other trail users: None, though tracks in the dirt indicate that mountain bikers have poached the route.
Canine compatibility: Leashed dogs permitted.
Fees and permits: Day-use fee charged at the Granite Bay entrance station
Schedule: Open 6:00 a.m. to 9:00 p.m. in the summer months (during daylight savings time); 7:00 a.m. to 7:00 p.m. in winter (during standard time)
Maps: USGS Rocklin; Folsom Lake State Recreation Area map available at park entry stations and online
Trail contact: Folsom Lake State Recreation Area, 7755 Folsom-Auburn Road, Folsom 95630; (916) 988-0205; www.parks .ca.gov
Special considerations: When the lake level is high, the latter part of the trail may be underwater, making a loop impossible. In that case, return as you came.

The park is home to rattlesnakes and mountain lions. Use caution and common sense when hiking in the area. Report wildcat sightings to park rangers.

Avoid contact with poison oak, which thrives in the woodland, by staying on the trail.
Additional information: Trail-

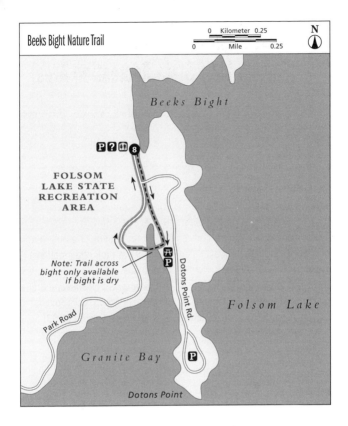

Beeks Bight Nature Trail

0 Kilometer 0.25

0 Mile 0.25

N

Beeks Bight

P ? 🚻 8

**FOLSOM
LAKE STATE
RECREATION
AREA**

*Note: Trail across
bight only available
if bight is dry*

A P

Dotons Point Rd.

Folsom Lake

Park Road

Granite Bay

P

Dotons Point

head amenities include rest-rooms, trash cans, parking, and information boards. Folsom Lake State Recreation Area attracts millions of visitors each year and offers a variety of outdoor activities, including boating, windsurf-ing, swimming, fishing, camping, picnicking, cycling and mountain biking, horseback riding, and lounging on the beach. Much more information is available on the park Web site.

Finding the trailhead: From Interstate 80 east of Sacramento (in Roseville), take the Douglas Road exit. Go 5.3 miles to the intersection of Douglas Road and Auburn-Folsom Road; continue on Douglas Road for 1 mile to the Granite Bay entrance station. From the entrance station, follow the park road for 3.8 miles to its end at the Beeks Bight trailhead parking area. The trailhead is in the southeast corner of the parking area, near the information boards. *DeLorme Northern California Atlas & Gazetteer:* Page 87 B5. GPS: N38 46.150 / W121 7.957

The Hike

In the height of summer, Folsom Lake attracts recreationalists like the bell of an ice-cream truck attracts children. Boaters and swimmers, campers and picnickers, horseback riders and mountain bikers—they congregate on the water and along the shoreline, savoring the expansive scenery, the abundant opportunities for fun and thrills, and whatever is cooking on the outdoor grill.

Hikers may be challenged to find peace and quiet on even the remotest of the park's 95 miles of trail during the summer. The nature trail at Beeks Bight is no exception. But in the off-season, when temperatures cool and the boats are stored, you stand a good chance of being downright isolated on this singletrack excursion.

Interpretive panels along the route, placed by local schoolchildren in 2002, offer insight into the human and natural history of the oak woodland ecosystem you'll traverse. They describe how native tribes used the resources of the woodlands, including how different varieties of oak were used as medicine, food, and dye; how soaproot was used; and how fire benefits the environment. The trail also is lined with numbered markers; check for guides at the

Granite Bay entrance station. You'll also find benches along the path, perfect for a rest or a snack.

The first interpretive panel, encountered at the trail-head, defines "bight" as a bay or cove—in this case a cove named for miller Joe Beek. The bight may be empty or full, depending on the lake level. In late season 2008 it was bone dry to near its mouth, allowing hikers to traverse a grassy valley that might otherwise have been underwater.

The path begins by wandering through oak woodlands along the edge of the bight. Birds flit in and out of the scrub, making this a popular site for birders; wildflowers bloom in season in pockets of grasslands between the thickets. You'll emerge from the woodland to views of Folsom Lake and Folsom Dam in the distance (an interpretive sign describes the dam's purpose and benefits). The path merges with a bike trail near the mouth of the bight, climbing gently to trail's end at a small gravel parking area on Dotons Point Road.

If the bight is full, retrace your steps to the trailhead. If it's not, return to the trail junction in the meadow and stay left, following the well-worn social trail that crosses the dry bottom then climbs to the park road. Turn right (north) onto the road, which leads back to the trailhead.

Miles and Directions

0.0   Start behind the information board, heading right (south) past the interpretive sign that defines the bight. A mountain biking route departs to the left. Cross a bridge and head into the woodland.

0.1   Pass posts 3, 4, and 5 and cross Dotons Point Road. Continue straight (south) on the nature trail.

0.3   Pass a bench and some interesting rock outcrops. A graveled patch of trail reaches from post 12 to post 13.

0.4 Picnic tables overlook a lovely meadow studded with granite outcrops when the bight is dry. Continue south, enjoying views of the lake and dam.

0.5 The nature trail merges with a multiuse singletrack. Go left (southeast) on the blended trail, gently climbing to trail's end at Dotons Point Road. A small parking area and trash cans are available here. If the bight is full, return as you came. If not, return to the trail junction and go left (northwest), across the bottom of the bight.

0.6 Social trails merge in the bottomlands; stay right on the most well worn track and climb toward a trail marker.

0.7 Climb up to the park road and turn right (north).

1.1 Arrive back at the trailhead and parking area.

9 Loop Trail (Gibson Ranch County Park)

The relative wildness of the Dry Creek riparian corridor and a patch of bird-filled marshland bookend pastures and paddocks at Gibson Ranch County Park.

Distance: 3.0-mile loop
Approximate hiking time: 1.5 hours
Difficulty: Moderate
Trail surface: Dirt singletrack, dirt ranch road, a short stretch on the roadside
Best season: Year-round
Other trail users: Equestrians, trail runners
Canine compatibility: Leashed dogs permitted
Fees and permits: Day-use fee
Schedule: Open from sunrise to sunset daily
Maps: USGS Rio Linda; park map available at the entry kiosk
Trail contact: Sacramento County Regional Parks Department, 3711 Branch Center Road, Sacramento 95827; (916) 875-6961; www.msa2.saccounty.net/parks; information on equestrian activities at the working ranch: www.gibson-ranch.com
Special considerations: No water is available along the trail, so bring all you need.
Additional information: There are no amenities at the trailhead proper other than parking, but nearby picnic areas have restrooms and water. The park is a working ranch and accommodates a number of activities, including picnicking, trail rides, animal husbandry, and fishing. While you are welcome to explore all facets of the ranch, please do not feed the animals.

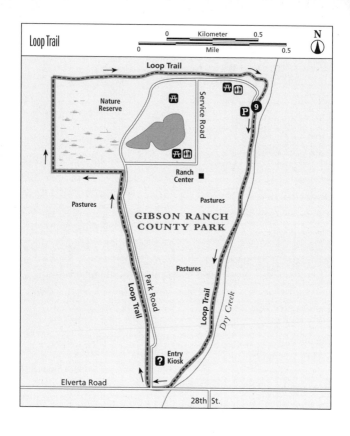

Loop Trail

Kilometer

Mile

N

Loop Trail

Nature Reserve

Service Road

P 9

Ranch Center

Pastures

Pastures

GIBSON RANCH COUNTY PARK

Pastures

Park Road

Loop Trail

Loop Trail

Dry Creek

Entry Kiosk

Elverta Road

28th St.

Finding the trailhead: From Interstate 80, the Capitol City Free-way (Business 80), or U.S. Highway 50, take the Watt Avenue exit. Head north on Watt Avenue to Elverta Road (about 5 miles from the I-80 exit). Turn left (west) onto Elverta Road and follow it for 0.7 mile to the park entrance on the right (north). The park road leads 1.3 miles past a number of pastures and picnic areas, as well as the park store and the residential facilities, to the parking lot in the northeast corner of the property, along Dry Creek. The trailhead is marked by a couple of yellow posts at the base of the creek levee. *DeLorme Northern California Atlas & Gazetteer:* Page 86 B3. GPS: N38 43.644 / W121 23.912

The Hike

A circumnavigation of Gibson Ranch captures in a snapshot the meshing of natural, agricultural, and suburban worlds. The richness of the riparian zone along Dry Creek backs up to pastures and paddocks, pastures back up to the fenced-off backyards of neighborhood homes, and a birdsong-filled marsh backs up to farm roads and a radio tower. The park's perimeter trail encompasses all this diversity and more.

The route begins in the Dry Creek riparian corridor, a northwestern Sacramento greenbelt that is the subject of ongoing restoration efforts and plans to extend a multiuse path along its length. Contrary to its name, Dry Creek runs year-round. Within the park it is an inviting waterway bordered by oaks, cottonwoods, buckeyes, and tangled figs. Side trails drop to sandy beaches where you can wade or skip stones. On the other side of the path, fenced pastures and lowing cows are screened by trees and brush.

The suburban interface is up next, when the trail bumps against a golf course and Elverta Road, then traces the park access road along the fences of a neighboring subdivision. This segment ends at the pastures and paddocks of the ranch's robust population of horses. They've cropped the grasses in their enclosures to dirt, and some hug the fences, leveling big-eyed gazes on passing hikers.

The pastures end where the marsh begins—an expanse of reeds, cattails, willows, and cottonwoods that resounds with birdcall and provides respite from what can be an unrelenting sun. A radio tower rises in the northwest corner of the park at the marsh's border, and a fence separates the ranch from adjacent private land. The final stretch of trail skirts the picnic areas surrounding the park's lake, the scene complete with playing greens and barbecues.

Ranching has a long history in California, including the Sacramento Valley. Spanish colonizers, and later Mexican dons, ran cattle on vast *ranchos* throughout what was then known as Alta California. The animals provided hides, tallow, and meat for their owners. Though the gold rush and California's eventual inclusion in the United States resulted in huge cultural changes, one thing has remained constant in areas where the grass grows thick and nutritious: ranching.

At Gibson Ranch horses dominate, but the ranch also supports cattle, goats, llamas, and smaller farm animals like chickens and rabbits. The park hosts school groups, horse camps, trail rides, and Civil War reenactments, as well as birthday parties and group picnics. It can be a busy place, but early mornings and weekdays offer the possibility for some solitude along the loop trail.

Miles and Directions

0.0 Start by heading right (south) on the shady elevated trail along Dry Creek. Social trails drop to the creek, and park amenities including soccer fields and parking lots are visible through the trees and shrubs on the right (west).

0.2 At the trail junction stay straight (south) on the obvious creekside route.

0.5 At the intersection continue straight (south) on the creek trail, passing a shelter at the edge of a fenced pasture. The trees thin, offering views downstream from sandbar to sandbar.

0.8 The trail curves west to another trail junction. You can see the neighboring golf links and hear cars passing on nearby Elverta Road. Continue straight on the loop trail.

1.0 The trail meets Elverta Road. Head west alongside the road to the park road, then turn north, following the edge of the road past the entry kiosk and hooking up with a dirt track parallel to the roadway. Homes border the trail on the left (west).

1.5 Pastures border both sides of the road and trail. Continue north.

1.7 Arrive at the stop sign at the junction of the park road and the road to the park store. Go left (west) on the dirt road that passes between Pastures 16 and 10. Horse paddocks border the track.

2.0 Reach the park boundary and turn left (north) onto the ranch road that skims the edge of the marsh. Oaks shade the route, and thick willows and reeds erupt from the wetlands. Algae-covered pools give way gradually to meadows that bloom with wildflowers in season.

2.2 The radio tower and a fence mark the park's northwest boundary. Go right (east) on the dirt road toward the ranch buildings and pastures.

2.6 The trail reaches the park road then parallels it past the picnic grounds and tot lots bordering the lake.

2.7 Pass an intersection of park roads at Picnic Area 3.

2.9 Pass a gate and climb onto the Dry Creek Trail at the park's northeastern boundary. Go right (south) on the trail.

3.0 Arrive back at the trailhead and parking lot.

10 Effie Yeaw Nature Loop (Ancil Hoffman County Park)

Wander interpretive trails through oak woodlands populated with deer, wild turkeys, and an abundance of birdlife to a scenic stretch of the American River.

Distance: 1.5-mile loop

Approximate hiking time: 1 hour

Difficulty: Easy

Trail surface: Dirt singletrack

Best season: Year-round, though summertime heat and winter storms may preclude pleasant hiking

Other trail users: None

Canine compatibility: Dogs not permitted

Fees and permits: None; donations gratefully accepted

Schedule: Open sunrise to sunset daily

Maps: USGS Carmichael; free trail maps available in the Effie Yeaw Interpretive Center

Trail contact: Sacramento County Regional Parks Department, 3711 Branch Center Road, Sacramento 95827; (916) 875-6961; www.msa2.saccounty.net/parks; Effie Yeaw Nature Center: (916) 489-4918

Special considerations: Avoid contact with poison oak and ticks by staying on trails. Rattlesnakes and mountain lions may be found on the nature center property. Encounters are unlikely, but familiarize yourself with proper behavior should you encounter either wild creature.

Additional information: Trailhead amenities include an information board and plenty of parking. Restrooms are in the Effie Yeaw Interpretive Center. No water is available along the trail, so bring all you need.

The Effie Yeaw Interpretive Center is well worth a visit. The center houses informative displays that are both adult and kid friendly. The center is open 9:00 a.m. to 5:00 p.m. daily February through October; 9:30 a.m. to 4:00 p.m. November through January. It is closed on Thanksgiving, Christmas Day, and New Year's Day.

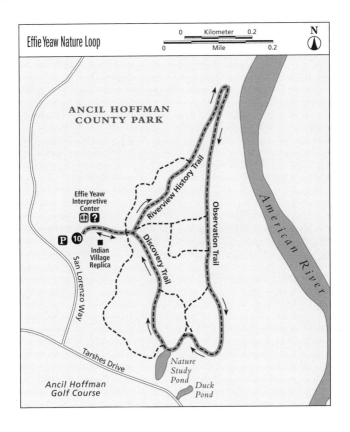

Kilometer

Mile

N

ANCIL HOFFMAN
COUNTY PARK

Effie Yeaw
Interpretive
Center

Indian
Village
Replica

San Lorenzo Way

Riverview History Trail

Observation Trail

Discovery Trail

American River

Tarshes Drive

Ancil Hoffman
Golf Course

Nature
Study
Pond

Duck
Pond

Finding the trailhead: From U.S. Highway 50, take the Watt Avenue exit. Go north for 1.8 miles on Watt Avenue to Fair Oaks Boulevard. Turn right (east) onto Fair Oaks and go 4 miles to Van Alstine Avenue. Go right (east) on Van Alstine Avenue for 0.4 mile to California Avenue and turn left (north). Follow California for 0.1 mile to Tarshes Drive and the entrance to Ancil Hoffman County Park. Follow Tarshes Drive for 1 mile, through the golf course, to San Lorenzo Way. Turn left (north) onto San Lorenzo Way and go 0.2 mile to the interpretive center parking area and trailhead. *DeLorme Northern California Atlas & Gazetteer:* Pages 86 and 87 D4. GPS: N38 37.015 / W121 18.758

The Hike

Walk this trail with the web of life in mind. Everything is connected: the river to the shore, the shore to the trees, the trees to the wind, the wind to the wings of the hawk that flies overhead. A quote from Chief Seattle, posted in the Effie Yeaw Interpretive Center, helps set the tone:

> *Man did not weave the web of life;*
> *He is merely a strand in it.*
> *Whatever he does to the web, he does to himself.*

Every hike on this nature loop should begin with a visit to the interpretive center, which houses a bonanza of information about the natural and human history of the American River basin. The center houses a room full of stations describing the ecology and natural history of the area, including touchable displays (such as condor wings that you can try on), a living saw-whet owl and great horned owl, and native snakes, including a garter snake, king snake, and rattlesnake. You can also pick up guidebooks that will help you identify these creatures and more wherever you travel.

The center and trails are named for teacher Effie Yeaw, who, according to park literature, led local schoolchildren on nature walks through what was then known as Deterding Woods. She also spearheaded a number of efforts to preserve the American River Parkway, recognizing its potential as both a natural and cultural landmark. Her legacy shines along these trails, which interpret the human and ecological history of the river.

Paths intertwine on the nature center property, enabling hikers to vary the route to suit their whim. A clockwise loop around the nature study area is described here, beginning with a tour of the re-created Nisenan village and native plantings around the nature center. The route then heads north along the Riverview History Trail to the banks of the American River.

Follow the river south on the Observation Trail, skimming the interface between its cobbled banks and the oak woodlands that thrive on its shores. The Discovery Trail leads back north toward the interpretive center, passing the nature study pond that offers hikers the opportunity to sit and watch the ducks ply the still waters. Interpretive signs along all the trails offer insights into the history and natural diversity preserved here.

Though paths are lined with interpretive signs, it's not always clear what trail you are on, as other trails frequently intercept the route. If you get confused or stray, don't worry: The area is small enough and well traveled enough that you won't get lost. Variations on these mingling trails are numerous, so wander at will.

The interconnectedness of the place, even to surrounding suburbia, is not subtle. If a question lingers, consider that deer in the park are absolutely fearless, foraging the annual grasses with little or no regard for hikers passing on the trails. Standing close to these wild creatures, with the boundaries of predator and prey broken by time and development, is a perfect demonstration of how changes on one strand in the web of life affect those occupying another strand.

Miles and Directions

0.0 Start by exploring the Nisenan village cultural demonstration area, where tule huts, a granary, and other native California artifacts have been replicated. Native plantings, identified with signs, line the gravel path.

0.1 The Discovery and Riverview History Trails begin on the south side of the interpretive center and Indian village. Head east on the broad dirt path, which is lined with interpretive signs. The Riverview History Trail documents human history in the area, and the Discovery Trail describes local habitats.

0.3 The Riverview History and Discovery Trails split amid a cluster of trail intersections. Stay left (northeast) on the broad Riverview History Trail.

0.4 Stay straight at the next unsigned trail intersection, heading northwest toward the river.

0.5 Turn right (east) on the narrow track that leads down to the unsigned singletrack Observation Trail above the river; there is a bench at the intersection. Turn right (south), headed downstream along the border of the riparian zone. Social trails lead down onto the cobbled floodplain; stay high on the well-trod trail lined with interpretive signs, feasting on river views.

0.7 Pass interpretive marker 7, which describes how hydraulic mining in the river devastated the ecosystem before it was outlawed.

0.8 At the trail junction stay straight (south and parallel to the river), heading into the woodland.

1.0 Pass a bench dedicated to Col. Bill Dula and stay left (south) along the river. The trail enters an open grassland.

1.1 At the signed junction for trails to the nature center and the nature study pond, go right (north) on the pond route (the Discovery Trail).

1.2 Turn left (west) to the reed-rimmed pond, where you'll find a couple of benches and an interpretive sign that describes the pond's purpose. When you've finished watching the ducks, head north on the signed trail to the nature center.

1.3 Pass a bench and trail sign.

1.4 Stay left (north) at the trail junction, passing interpretive signs that describe the ecosystem at the woodland's edge and then passing wild grapes.

1.5 Arrive back at the junction with the Riverview History Trail at an interpretive sign about redbud. Turn left (west) to return to the nature center and trailhead.

11 Jedediah Smith Memorial Trail and Discovery Park (American River Parkway)

This sampling of Sacramento's premier trail begins at the confluence of the American and Sacramento Rivers and stretches east through manicured parklands and strips of relatively untouched riparian woodlands.

Distance: 4.4 miles out and back

Approximate hiking time: 2.5 hours

Difficulty: Moderate due to length

Trail surface: Paved

Best season: Year-round; the trailhead area at the confluence may flood in winter or with spring runoff.

Other trail users: Cyclists (lots of them), trail runners, in-line skaters and skateboarders, equestrians

Canine compatibility: Leashed dogs permitted

Fees and permits: $5 fee at Discovery Park. Fees are levied at other American River Parkway access points, although neighborhood access generally is free.

Schedule: Open from sunrise to sunset daily

Maps: USGS Sacramento East and Sacramento West. A Jedediah Smith Memorial Bicycle Trail map produced by the Sacramento County Regional Parks Department is available for purchase at various locations along the trail, including the Effie Yeaw Interpretive Center in Ancil Hoffman County Park, and at www.msa2.saccounty.net/parks.

Trail contact: Sacramento County Regional Parks Department, 3711 Branch Center Road, Sacramento 95827; (916) 875-6961; www.msa2.saccounty.net/parks

Special considerations: This trail is extremely popular with cyclists. The speed limit is 15 miles per

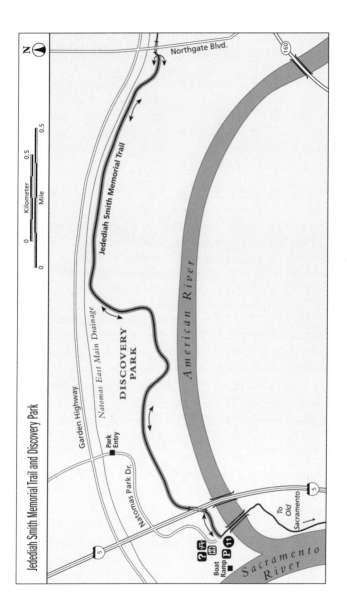

Jedediah Smith Memorial Trail and Discovery Park

hour but it is not always obeyed. Stay to the right as you walk, allowing bikers plenty of room to pass. Most cyclists will warn of their approach.

Summertime temperatures can zoom into the 100s, so bring plenty of drinking water.

Additional information: Amenities at Discovery Park include parking, restrooms, informational boards, water, picnic facilities, and a boat launch. There are no amenities at the Northgate Boulevard turnaround. Call boxes are located along the route.

Finding the trailhead: Discovery Park is in the shadow of Interstate 5 just north of the state capitol and Capitol Mall. Take the Garden Highway exit from I-5 and follow the Garden Highway east for 0.4 mile to the Discovery Park entrance. The boat ramp and trailhead are located in the west end of the park at the confluence. *DeLorme Northern California Atlas & Gazetteer:* Page 86 D2. GPS: N38 36.024 / W121 30.455

The Hike

The American River Parkway, a linear greenbelt that stretches from downtown Sacramento to Folsom Lake, is without question the most loved open space in the Sacramento region. If the American River is the parkway's anchor, then the 32-mile paved Jedediah Smith Memorial Trail is the chain that links the river to the hearts of the people.

To explore the length of the memorial trail on foot would require days—a feat worthy of the trail's mountaineering namesake, Jedediah Smith, who hiked across the Sierra in the early 1800s and camped along the river. Taken in segments, however, the trail easily accommodates six to eight great easy day hikes. You could explore the confluence of the Sacramento and American Rivers at Discovery

Park one day, move upstream to check out the exposed protected area at Cal Expo the next, then spend another day on the riverfront in Pond and Goethe Parks. Farther upstream, the trail passes through the Lower and Upper Sunrise areas, rambling through oak woodlands with wonderful river views to the Nimbus Dam and fish hatchery. A circuit of Lake Natoma would make a pleasant daylong outing. And then there's a link along the shoreline of Folsom Lake . . .

The trail through Discovery Park is the focus of this trail description, beginning at the dynamic confluence of the Sacramento and American Rivers. This area is busy in spring, summer, and fall, with boats launching into the swift-moving waterways, folks crowding picnic grounds and fishing from the riverbanks, hikers and cyclists heading out on the trail, and archers practicing their skills at the archery range. The trail then wanders along a relatively quiet stretch through the river's floodplain in the shade of oaks and sycamores, with interpretive signs scattered trailside offering insight into the riparian habitat and the creatures that live there. The turnaround point is Northgate Boulevard, but you can continue on . . . and on . . .

I urge you to consider the following options for additional day hikes, which are described here with shameful brevity. Visit www.msa2.saccounty.net/parks for directions and additional information.

- The 4.0-mile out-and-back stretch of trail between Watt Avenue (where you'll find parking) and the Guy West pedestrian suspension bridge (a scaled-down Golden Gate Bridge) is bounded by quiet neighborhoods and the scenic river. Parallel trails include a dirt track at the foot of the levee and a levee-top path.

- Pick up the trail in William B. Pond Recreation Area and head east, across the scenic Jedediah Smith pedestrian bridge, into C. M. Goethe Park. Both parks offer all kinds of amenities, including picnic areas, playing greens, and river frontage. This is a little more than 2.0 miles out and back. If you continue into the more undeveloped areas of Goethe Park, the trail traverses oak woodlands and savanna that can be hot and exposed in summer.

- A scenic gorge, the lovely Fair Oaks pedestrian bridge, great river views and access, and the shade of overhanging oaks recommend the 4.0-mile out-and-back trail segment between the Upper Sunrise access point and the Nimbus Fish Hatchery at Hazel Avenue.

Miles and Directions

0.0 Start near the boat launch and the I-5 overpass, where yellow posts mark the trailhead. Pass under the freeway and head east along the American River past lawns and picnic areas shaded by sycamores.

0.4 Noise from the freeway fades as fields and parking lots open on the left (north).

0.6 Pass the archery range on the left (north). As you enter the riparian woodland, an interpretive sign describes the trail and the cottonwood forest that surrounds you.

0.8 Pass an interpretive sign about habitat restoration.

1.3 Reach a stop sign where the Jedediah Smith Trail meets a paved access trail. Continue straight (east) on the Jedediah Smith Trail. The river is out of sight to the right (south), separated from the trail by the grassy floodplain.

1.9 Pass a call box. A huge hedge of blackberry shields a utility yard on the right (south), then the floodplain opens again.

Power lines trace the route, and you may spy a kite perched on the wire, looking for tasty rodents in the field below. The paved route is shadowed by a gravel track. On the left a water-filled channel (the Natomas East Main Drainage) supports a thick riparian ribbon.

2.2 Reach the Northgate Boulevard trail junction and the turn-around point. Retrace your steps toward the confluence.

4.4 Arrive back at the trailhead and parking area.

12 Old Sacramento and Capitol Promenade

A boardwalk and promenade along the Sacramento River waterfront leads from historic Old Sacramento, with its shops, restaurants, and museums, to Tower Bridge, Capitol Mall, and the edge of downtown.

Distance: 1.1 miles out and back
Approximate hiking time: 1 hour (if you don't stop to enjoy the sights for too long)
Difficulty: Easy
Trail surface: Paved, boardwalk
Best season: Year-round
Other trail users: Cyclists
Canine compatibility: Leashed dogs permitted
Fees and permits: None
Schedule: Open day and night year-round
Maps: USGS Sacramento West
Trail contact: Ed Cox, Bicycle and Pedestrian Coordinator, City of Sacramento, 915 I Street, Room 2000, Sacramento 95814; (916) 808-8434
Special considerations: Parking is either on the street or in parking garages. The garage at the end of J Street is closest to the trailhead. Parking fees are levied.
Additional information: Bring your pocketbook so you can purchase entry to one of the museums along the trail or enjoy a meal in a waterfront restaurant. And then there's the shopping . . .

Finding the trailhead: The trailhead is located along the Sacramento River behind the California State Railroad Museum and Sacramento Discovery Museum in Old Sacramento. Take the J Street exit from Interstate 5 and follow the signs to Old Sacramento. Both on-street parking and parking garages are available in the area; fees are charged. The closest garage is across the street from the railroad museum, which is located at 111 I Street. *DeLorme Northern California Atlas & Gazetteer:* Page 86 D2. GPS: N38 35.058 / W121 30.256

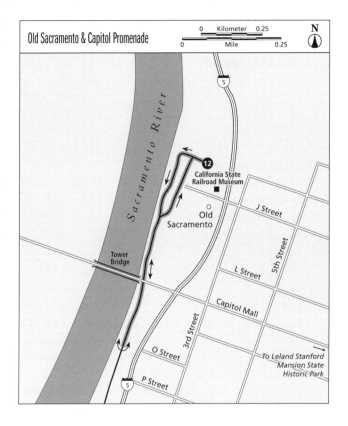

0   Kilometer   0.25

0   Mile   0.25

N

Sacramento River

5

12
California State
Railroad Museum

J Street

5th Street

Old
Sacramento

Tower
Bridge

L Street

Capitol Mall

3rd Street

O Street

To Leland Stanford
Mansion State
Historic Park

P Street

5

The Hike

Culture and history collide with great scenery along this short urban route. Sandwiched between the Sacramento River and a working rail line in the heart of California's capital city, the trail lacks nothing: It serves up restaurants, riverboat rides, tattoo parlors, candy shops, a history lesson, and the chance to see an old-time locomotive cruising on a historic set of tracks.

The trail begins where the rail line begins, in front of the historic Central Pacific Railroad Depot in Old Sacramento. It traces the tracks of the working Sacramento Southern Railroad, upon which the California State Railroad Museum runs excursion trains from April to September. The railroad dates back to the turn of the twentieth century, when the Southern Pacific built the line to facilitate transportation of the bounty of the Central Valley's fields and orchards to port cities in the Bay Area.

The Sacramento River bounds the trail on the west side, flowing broad and deep as it connects the Gold Country to San Francisco. The trail offers views down onto boats plying the quick waters, which look deceptively smooth but harbor powerful currents. This is no place for a swim.

A rustic boardwalk leads south past touristy restaurants and the *Delta King* paddleboat, ending at the intersection with Capitol Mall. The yellow pylons of Tower Bridge rise on the right (west), and the capitol building graces the end of the mall on the left (east).

Carefully cross the road and continue south along the wide, lighted promenade lined with lampposts and flower-filled planters bearing plaques that describe Sacramento's colorful history. River travel and locomotives, wharves and warehouses; food-packing plants and laundry houses: You can read all about it. Benches overlook the river, making this the perfect place to rest and digest after a meal in one of the downtown restaurants. The glass-faced high-rises of the downtown area rise on one side and the glassy river flows on the other, making the whole scene brilliant on a sunny day.

The hike concludes at the Circle of Lights Plaza at the intersection of Front and O Streets, where a collection of streetlights from the city of Sacramento is displayed. A bike trail continues from the end of the promenade, leading south along the river to Sacramento's Miller Park and Marina. Plans call for the extension of the promenade along this route, replacing the bike trail, with construction slated for 2009. Until construction is complete, the end of the promenade is the turnaround point. Return as you came, taking a detour to explore the shops and cafes housed in the colorful buildings of the historic district.

Miles and Directions

0.0 Start on the riverfront levee, heading south on the top of the levee between the railroad tracks and the river. You'll pass a few interpretive signs as you ramble beneath the sycamores.

0.1 The wide boardwalk begins. Pass the *Delta King* paddleboat and the railroad depot, with Tower Bridge looming ahead.

0.4 Arrive at the junction with Capitol Mall. Cross the street and continue on the promenade.

0.5 The promenade ends at Front and O Streets. Retrace your steps to Old Sacramento.

1.1 Take a detour through the historic district, returning to the trailhead near the railroad museum.

Option: To visit the state capitol (also a state park), go southeast along the Capitol Mall from the foot of Tower Bridge to the copper-domed capitol building. On the capitol grounds you'll find a museum, gardens, and memorials. For more information visit www.parks.ca.gov and select "California State Capitol Museum."

13 Mather Nature Loops (Mather Rotary Regional Recreation Area)

A pair of short loops ramble alongside Mather Lake, offering hikers a chance to stretch their legs, learn about the local habitat, and visit vernal pools in spring.

Distance: 1.5 miles of interlocking loops
Approximate hiking time: 1 hour
Difficulty: Easy
Trail surface: Wide dirt and gravel trails
Best season: Winter and spring to view the vernal pools; fall for color
Other trail users: None
Canine compatibility: Leashed dogs permitted
Fees and permits: Parking fee
Schedule: Open sunrise to sunset daily
Maps: USGS Carmichael
Trail contact: Sacramento County Regional Parks Department, 3711 Branch Center Road, Sacramento 95827; (916) 875-6961; www.msa2.saccounty.net/parks

Special considerations: Summer temperatures may preclude use of these trails at midday, and winter rains may render the trails muddy.

Additional information: Trailhead amenities include ample parking, restrooms, water, a tot lot, lawns, trash cans, and a fishing pier. The lake is stocked with black bass and trout; no motorized boats are allowed. No trail maps are available, but trails around the lake are short and straightforward. The vernal pools fill in winter, bloom in April and early May, and are gone by late May.

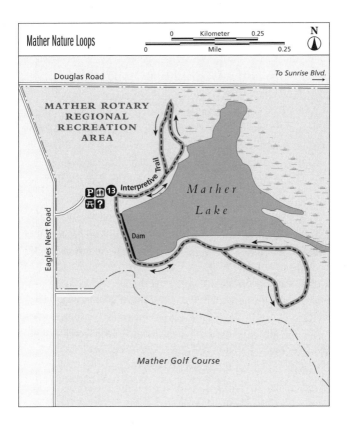

Mather Nature Loops

0   Kilometer   0.25

0   Mile   0.25

N

Douglas Road

To Sunrise Blvd.

MATHER ROTARY
REGIONAL
RECREATION
AREA

Interpretive Trail

Mather Lake

Eagles Nest Road

Dam

Mather Golf Course

Finding the trailhead: From U.S. Highway 50 take the Sunrise Boulevard exit. Head south onto Sunrise Boulevard to Douglas Road and turn right (west). Follow Douglas Road for 1 mile to Eagles Nest Road and turn left (south). Follow Eagles Nest Road for 0.3 mile to the signed park entrance on the left (east). The trailhead for the first loop is on the south side of the lake, behind the gate on the dam. The interpretive loop begins to the left (northeast), behind the picnic pavilion. *DeLorme Northern California Atlas & Gazetteer:* Page 87 D4. GPS: N38 33.415 / W121 15.572

The Hike

The planes may come and the planes may go, but some things will stay the same at Mather Field. Grasslands that once were part of an Air Force base are now a sprawling regional park—a place where migrating and resident birds, rare and fragile creatures in vernal pools, and appreciative hikers can abide and revive.

Though suburbia encroaches on all sides, and the roar of aircraft engines and freeway traffic nixes this as a wilderness experience, the abundance of color and wildlife makes a visit to Mather Lake more than worthwhile. It's the perfect outing for a family, where you can mix hiking with fishing, a picnic, a romp on the tot lot . . . and, for older "kids," perhaps a round of golf.

You'll find ducks and geese on the lake year-round, but visit during spring or fall if you are interested in species that migrate along the Pacific Flyway. Autumn is lovely, as the green foliage of willows, cottonwoods, and other riparian plants around the lake morphs to gold. Spring is even more colorful: That's when the vernal pools bloom, with blankets of meadowfoam and goldfields thrown briefly across depressions in the grasslands that disappear within weeks.

The vernal pools also enliven a winter visit to the park. A unique and precious environment, the plants and animals that inhabit the pools are, in many cases, rare and endangered. These include fairy shrimp, which survive the long dry season as cysts, then hatch and reproduce in the brief time the pool is full. Visit www.sacsplash.org/mather.htm for links to in-depth descriptions of plants and animals found in vernal pools.

Mather Lake was once part of Mather Air Force Base.

Named for World War I test pilot Carl Mather, the airfield dates back to 1918 and was operational through World War II, the Cold War, and the Vietnam War. The base closed in 1995, and the property was divided into a county airport and parkland. Development of the park is ongoing, with a coalition of community groups, including the Audubon Society and the Rotary Club, balancing preservation of open spaces with more intensive uses like ball fields.

The tour of trails around Mather Lake is described beginning with the loop on the south shore, then the nature trail on the northwest shore, but you can take them in any order. The first loop explores the riparian zone and grasslands, with access to waterside picnic sites. The second loop follows a short interpretive trail, where signs describe the area's creatures, from frogs to rodents, and the habitat that nurtures them.

Miles and Directions

0.0 Start behind the gate that blocks vehicle access to the dam. Follow the dam south, with the lake on your left and meadowland to the right.

0.1 At the end of the dam (which borders the fenced Mather Golf Course), go left (east) on the dirt track, dropping through a picnic site.

0.3 The trail splits; stay right (east). At the second split stay right (east) again, heading into the meadow.

0.5 Swing north as the trail approaches the fence that separates the golf course from the natural area. Marshland thick with cattails and reeds borders the route on the right (north), and birdcall emanating from the bush almost overcomes the rumble of traffic.

0.7 The trail loops back on itself along the lakeshore. Retrace your steps back to the trailhead.

1.0 Arrive at the parking area. Pick up the trail on the northwest shore of the lake, passing the fishing pier and a series of benches set in the trees at waterside. You'll also pass an information sign that details the history of Mather Field.

1.1 The nature trail splits. Go right on the lakeside track, following the line of interpretive signs through the riparian thickets.

1.3 The trail merges onto a wider track near a gate that bars access to nearby Douglas Road. Turn left (southwest) on the gravel road, heading back toward the picnic area through a grassland dotted with adolescent oaks and sycamores.

1.4 Reach the split in the nature trail and, unless you want to do laps, retrace your steps toward the trailhead.

1.5 Arrive back at the trailhead and parking area.

14 Outer Loop Trail (South Fork Putah Creek Regional Preserve)

Tucked against the banks of Putah Creek, this trail loop offers seclusion, bird watching, and a chance to check out the process of restoring agricultural land to native habitat.

Distance: 1.4-mile loop
Approximate hiking time: 1 hour
Difficulty: Easy
Trail surface: Wide dirt trails
Best season: Spring and fall. Summertime heat may limit trail use to mornings and evenings. Winter rains may render trails muddy; wait a couple of days and the surface will firm up.
Other trail users: None
Canine compatibility: Leashed dogs permitted
Fees and permits: No fees or permits required
Schedule: Open sunrise to sunset daily
Maps: USGS Davis; trail map on the information board at the trailhead
Trail contact: City of Davis Parks and General Services, 23 Russell Road, Davis 95616; (530) 757-5656; www.cityofdavis.org
Special considerations: You may encounter rattlesnakes on the site. They will only strike if threatened, so keep your distance. No water is available, so bring all that you'll need.
Additional information: Trailhead facilities include a small parking area, an information board with a trail map, and trash cans.

Finding the trailhead: From downtown Sacramento head west on Interstate 80 toward Davis. Take the Mace Boulevard exit. Travel 2.3 miles south on Mace Boulevard to the trailhead, which is on the left (east) side of the road. *DeLorme Northern California Atlas & Gazetteer:* Page 86 D1. GPS: N38 31.038 / W121 41.703

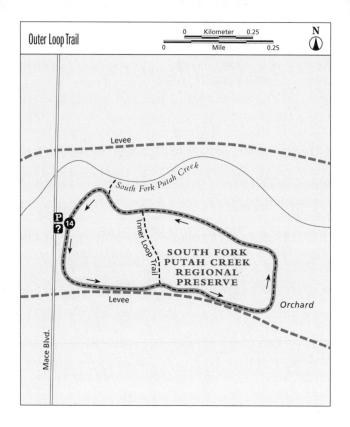

0   Kilometer   0.25
0   Mile   0.25

N

Levee

South Fork Putah Creek

P
? 14

Inner Loop Trail

**SOUTH FORK
PUTAH CREEK
REGIONAL
PRESERVE**

Levee

Orchard

Mace Blvd.

The Hike

The south fork of Putah Creek flows east from the coastal mountains north of San Francisco Bay into the Yolo Bypass Wildlife Area and the Sacramento River delta. The flow seems backward, but the creek eventually reaches its goal, the Pacific Ocean. Along the way, it waters farms and fields, contributing to the agricultural lifeblood of the Central Valley.

But in this preserve Putah Creek is allowed to flood, as it did before the arrival of Europeans, before levees and flood control canals, when the native Patwin lived and foraged along its banks. In this way it waters wetlands and riparian zones, once the dominant ecosystems in the area, and serves as the focus of rehabilitation efforts to transform a hundred-acre parcel from agricultural uses to natural habitat.

The man-made forces that have shaped the landscape for decades still envelop the preserve and its trails, with orchards neatly planted at its eastern boundary and an enormous levee bounding the south side. But as the information sign at the trailhead describes, the creek also supports a complex "riparian ribbon" that includes habitat for chinook salmon, prickly sculpin, California quail, and a variety of raptors. If all goes as planned, those creatures and the sycamores, willows, and oaks that foster them will find permanent renewal.

As of 2008 the restoration was still a work in progress. The riparian corridor along the creek itself, thick with berry brambles, cottonwoods, and willows, appeared healthy and complete—thick, green, and ringing with birdsong. By contrast, the meadow between the creekbanks and the levee was stark, with oaks just beginning to gain vigor and size amid annual grasses.

This pocket of parkland is isolated and relatively undiscovered, a huge bonus for the hiker seeking solitude. Visit in the morning or evening, or on any weekday, and you'll be alone with the birds chirping in the brush and the wind humming through the grasses. The trail is wide and easy to follow (though there are no trail signs). It begins with a visit to the creek, then heads east through savanna that blooms with sage and wildflowers such as wild rose and chamise in season. The loop bends south along the fenceline that separates the preserve from the orchard, then returns in the shadow of the levee. It's a walk-and-talk affair, perfect for families or friends seeking a quiet outing to catch up and, if so inclined, do a little bird watching.

Miles and Directions

0.0 Start by heading left (north) on the gravel trail.

0.1 At the trail intersection go left (north), toward the creek. The path leads a short distance down to the broad, quiet waterway. The bank is choked with berry brambles and poison oak, so while it's lovely to look at, it's not picnic-friendly. Return to the trail junction and go straight (south) on the broad trail.

0.3 Reach a junction with a road/trail at a fenceline; go left (east). The fence marks an inner boundary of what's natural and what still needs to be restored. At a second trail intersection (with the unsigned Inner Loop), stay straight (east), remaining on the unsigned Outer Loop. (**Option:** Turn right [south] onto the Inner Loop to shorten the hike to about 0.8 mile.)

0.6 At the junction stay straight (east) on the Outer Loop Trail. A rusted water trough sits outside the fence.

0.7 Circle south toward the levee. The property boundary is fenced on the left (east). Walk along the interface of the shaggy preserve and the orderly rows of the orchard.

0.8 Head westward along the foot of the levee, a sloping grassy wall that rises to the left (south).

1.0 Pass the junction with the Inner Loop and a gated roadway that leads up onto the levee. Stay straight (west) on the Outer Loop Trail.

1.3 Round the last curve of the loop, heading north parallel to Mace Boulevard toward the trailhead.

1.4 Arrive at the trailhead and parking area.

15 Cosumnes River Walk (Cosumnes River Preserve)

Meander through riparian thickets that border the Cosumnes River, the last unregulated river flowing from the western Sierra Nevada. The broad, slow waterway nourishes habitat for birds in remarkable number and variety.

Distance: 3.3 miles of interlocking loops

Approximate hiking time: 2 hours

Difficulty: Moderate due to trail length

Trail surface: Boardwalk, dirt singletrack, dirt road

Best season: Spring for wildflowers and bird migrations, fall for color and bird migrations

Other trail users: None

Canine compatibility: Dogs not permitted

Fees and permits: None, but donations welcome

Schedule: Open sunrise to sunset daily

Maps: USGS Bruceville; trail maps available at the Cosumnes River Preserve Visitor Center and at www.cosumnes.org

Trail contact: Cosumnes River Preserve, 13501 Franklin Boulevard, Galt 95632; (916) 684-2816; www.cosumnes.org

Special considerations: Although the Cosumnes River Walk is adequately signed and lined with interpretive posts, there are a number of options that may shorten or lengthen your tour. These options are not all signed and may be confusing. No worries; with the river as one landmark and the railroad tracks as another, you won't lose your way.

This trail description includes a detour that resulted from trail work in late 2008. Trail conditions may be different when trail work is complete.

The park is in mountain lion country. An encounter is unlikely, but use caution and common sense. Remain on the trail to avoid contact with poison oak and ticks.

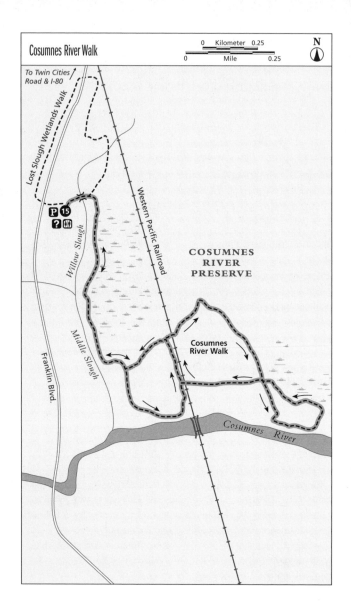

Cosumnes River Walk

0   Kilometer   0.25

0   Mile   0.25

N

To Twin Cities
Road & I-80

Lost Slough Wetlands Walk

Western Pacific Railroad

P 15

? 👥

Willow Slough

Middle Slough

Franklin Blvd.

COSUMNES
RIVER
PRESERVE

Cosumnes
River Walk

Cosumnes River

Additional information: Trailhead amenities include restrooms, water, and information kiosks. The visitor center (open weekends from 9:00 a.m. to 5:00 p.m. year-round and daily in July and August from 8:00 a.m. to noon) includes interpretive displays that describe the Cosumnes River ecosystem and the resident and migratory birds you might spot in the preserve. You'll also find interpretive publications and trail maps here.

Finding the trailhead: You can travel south from Sacramento to the preserve via either Interstate 5 or Highway 99. If traveling down I-5, take the Twin Cities Road exit and head east. Follow Twin Cities Road for 1 mile to Franklin Boulevard. Turn right (south) onto Franklin Boulevard and continue for 2 miles to the visitor center parking area on the left (east).

Alternatively, take Highway 99 south to the Twin Cities Road/Highway 104 exit. Go west on Twin Cities Road for 7.4 miles to the stop sign at Franklin Boulevard and turn left (south). Follow Franklin Boulevard to the preserve. *DeLorme Northern California Atlas & Gazetteer:* Page 96 B3. GPS: N38 15.933 / W121 26.430

The Hike

What does a free-flowing California river look like? The Cosumnes River, essentially unobstructed from its headwaters in the Sierra to where it empties into the Mokelumne River and ultimately the Sacramento River delta, will show you.

What thrives in the habitats that surround a free-flowing California river? The Cosumnes will show you that, too—from the sandhill cranes, ancient birds with a 7-foot wingspan that stop here in winter, to the riparian thickets and stands of valley oaks that crowd the riverbanks.

The Cosumnes River Preserve, established by The Nature Conservancy and Ducks Unlimited in 1987, protects a portion of the lower reaches of the river and its surrounding floodplain. This natural area includes freshwater wetlands; riparian zones that harbor cottonwoods, willows, and oaks; and meadowlands that bloom with wildflowers in season. The Cosumnes River Walk leads you into each of these lovely ecosystems.

Like all rivers, the 80-mile-long Cosumnes rises and subsides with the seasons, occasionally spilling out of its channel when swollen with snowmelt and rainfall. The flooding, typical of all Central Valley rivers before dams and levees contained them, deposited rich fertile soil in the valley bottom. Outside the preserve the bottomlands help feed the nation, supporting wildly productive farms. Within the preserve, soils support a diverse habitat that attracts large numbers and varieties of birds . . . which in turn attracts large numbers of bird-watchers. You don't have to be a birder to enjoy this walk—there are rodents, snakes, and lizards to spy; wildflowers to see and smell; and benches along a lazy river to rest and relax upon.

The Cosumnes River Walk begins on a boardwalk and a bridge that leads across the birdsong-filled Willow Slough. Lined with interpretive markers keyed to a guide available at the visitor center and online, the dirt trail heads south through a bower of tangled willow, cottonwood, wild rose, and berry brambles. The trail loops around and under the elevated tracks, leading to overlooks of the river. After the riverside visit, the loops lead though shady stands of oak, across valley oak savanna, and past a tule marsh.

The Cosumnes may not harbor a dam, but it is not untouched by development. The elevated Western Pacific Railroad tracks and the scenic railroad bridge that spans the river at the south end of the trail are one example; the hum of traffic from the nearby interstate, pervasive background noise to the birdcall, is another.

You may choose to do the two loops in a different order or in the opposite direction. The route described below takes the loop on the west side of the railroad tracks first, then the second loop on the east side, both in a counter-clockwise direction.

Miles and Directions

0.0   Start on the boardwalk north of the visitor center, which leads down and across the bridge over Willow Slough. Interpretive signs discuss how tides affect the slough.

0.1   The River Walk and the Wetlands Walk split. Go right (south) on the signed River Walk. The flat dirt track leads through the overgrown thickets that line the slough.

0.3   Reach a trail intersection. In 2008 a detour directed you left (east) on a maintenance road, then south along the tracks. If trail work is complete, continue straight (south) at this junction.

0.7   Reach a three-way trail intersection. Turn right (southwest), ignoring the trail that leads left (east) into the savanna and toward the elevated railroad tracks (you'll visit here later). The trail passes Marker 8 and follows the levee alongside Middle Slough.

1.0   The trail curves east along the riverbank, passing Markers 9 and 10 and a trail that leads to the riverside. A scenic railroad bridge spans the river as you approach the tracks.

1.2   The trail breaks out of the woodlands at a trail sign that describes invasive plants and animals. Head north on the broad roadway that parallels the elevated railroad tracks, passing the first trail that leads right (east) into the savanna. You will finish the second loop on this trail.

1.3 Go right (east), passing under the tracks and into the savanna.

1.5 Pass Marker 14 and a bench overlooking the marsh, then swing southeast through the meadow.

1.6 Cross a roadway and continue straight on the signed nature trail.

1.7 At the next intersection go right (south) on the signed nature trail.

1.8 At the four-way trail junction, go straight (south) toward the river.

1.9 A nature trail sign points you right on the riverside path. Circle through the trees, following the blue trail posts past Marker 12 and a series of benches overlooking the still waters of the broad, calm river.

2.0 Pass Marker 13 as the loop swings back to the west. Birdcall from the marsh to the right (north) can completely drown out any car noise you may hear.

2.2 The trail hops onto a levee and skims northwest through brambles toward the savanna.

2.3 Arrive back at the four-way trail junction. Go straight (west) toward the railroad tracks, passing Marker 11—about sedges used by natives in basket weaving—as you go.

2.5 Cross a road and pass under the tracks to the junction with the first trail loop. Turn right (north), parallel to the railroad tracks.

2.7 At the detour's junction turn left (west), crossing the meadow to link up with the first loop alongside Middle Slough. Go right (north), back toward the visitor center.

3.3 Arrive back at the trailhead and parking area.

Options: The paved Lost Slough Wetlands Walk, a 1.0-mile trek through the wetlands on the west side of Franklin Boulevard, offers the opportunity for further exploration of this lovely sanctuary.

16 Howard Ranch Trail (Rancho Seco Recreation Area)

This sprawling tour of the Rancho Seco Lake shoreline and a working cattle ranch offers a sampling of big-sky country in the Central Valley, with views stretching across the prairie to the Sierra Nevada. Vernal pools along the route bloom with wildflowers in season.

Distance: 6.9-mile lollipop
Approximate hiking time: 4 hours
Difficulty: More challenging due to length
Trail surface: Dirt singletrack, dirt ranch roads
Best season: Spring for the vernal pools; late fall for moderate temperatures and color along the lakeshore
Other trail users: None
Canine compatibility: No dogs permitted on the trail
Fees and permits: Parking fee
Schedule: Open at 7:00 a.m. daily; closing hours change seasonally, generally at sunset
Maps: USGS Goose Creek. A map and fact sheet can be downloaded from www.cosumnes .org/recreation/howard%20Trail.

pdf. Trail maps are also available at the Cosumnes River Preserve Visitor Center, located about 17 miles east of Rancho Seco at 13501 Franklin Boulevard in Galt.
Trail contact: Sacramento Municipal Utility District, 6301 S Street, Sacramento 95817 (mailing address: P.O. Box 15830, Sacramento 95852-1830); (888) 742-7683; www.smud.org; Rancho Seco Recreation Area: (209) 748-2318
Special considerations: This trail is long and remote. Be sure to bring plenty of drinking water and snacks.

You'll travel through a working cattle ranch. The cows you may encounter along the route are gentle creatures that will most

Howard Ranch Trail

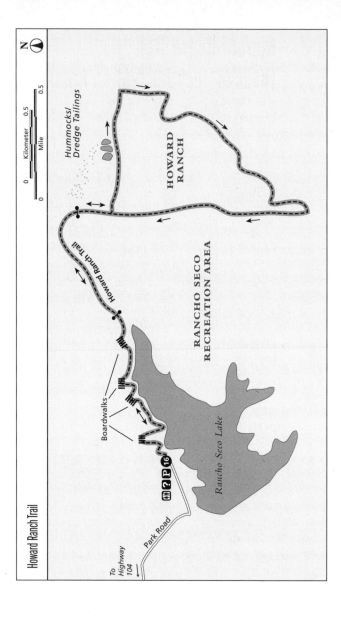

N

Kilometer
0   0.5
0   0.5
Mile

Hummocks/
Dredge Tailings

Howard Ranch Trail

HOWARD RANCH

RANCHO SECO
RECREATION AREA

Boardwalks

Rancho Seco Lake

To Highway 104

Park Road

likely scatter as you approach. Be sure to stay on trails and close all gates behind you. The park is also rattlesnake country. An encounter is unlikely, and the snakes won't attack unless threatened. Should you encounter one, keep your distance.

Additional information: Trailhead amenities include a restroom, trash cans, and an information board with a trail map.

Finding the trailhead: From Sacramento head south on Highway 99. Take the Twin Cities Road/Highway 104 exit and head east toward Jackson and Ione. Drive 13.9 miles through Herald and into Clay, staying left when the road splits at Clay East Road (which leads to Rancho Seco's decommissioned nuclear facility). The signed park entrance is on the right (south). Follow the access road for 0.3 mile to a left (east) turn into the park proper. Pass the entry kiosk and continue for 0.6 mile to a gravel road on the left that's signed for the Howard Ranch Trail. Follow the gravel road for 0.3 mile to the dirt parking lot. The trailhead is in the northeast corner of the lot at the information board. *DeLorme Northern California Atlas & Gazetteer:* Page 97 B5. GPS: N38 20.425 / W121 05.800

The Hike

The walls of river valleys and the trees of riparian zones hem in many trails in the Sacramento valley, but at Howard Ranch boundaries fall away. Save for the distant foothills of the Sierra Nevada, open range rolls in all directions, spotted with cattle and the occasional lonely oak or sycamore and seasonally abloom with wildflowers reflected in the still waters of vernal pools.

Those who crave cottonwoods, willows, and big water need never fear: This hike is not all big sky and big prairie. The trail begins as a sinuous meander along the tree-shrouded shoreline of Rancho Seco Lake. Gently curving, beautifully constructed boardwalks span seasonal streams feeding into the lake. In summer the lake and its camp-grounds bustle with visitors fishing, swimming, and boating. When the weather cools and the days shorten, it grows as quiet and calm as the grasslands that surround it.

The bulk of the hike is on the wide-open range. The Howard Ranch once belonged to Charles Howard, owner of the legendary racehorse Seabiscuit. Still a working ranch, it operates under a conservation easement that protects its rare ecosystems, including vernal pools. The vernal pools are a huge attraction—the subject of guided hikes and solitary explorations in winter, when they fill, and in spring, when they bloom. Rare and threatened species that abide in the ephemeral ponds include fairy shrimp, tadpole shrimp, and the California tiger salamander; wildflowers include vibrant spreads of goldfields and meadowfoam.

But I'd be remiss if I didn't mention the significant, pro-vocative tableau that looms over the ranch and lake. Rancho Seco's neighbor is a nuclear power plant, with two huge cooling towers rising from the flats on the west side of the park. For the most part the towers are out of sight, behind you as you walk east across the ranch and mostly hidden by grassy rises as you curve south and west—which is pretty amazing given their height and bulk. I wouldn't call them a detraction—they aren't unlovely, just unlikely. Instead I'd argue they add depth and complexity to the journey. No matter how you feel about nuclear power as a political or environmental issue, the towers spark the imagination and present the opportunity to consider the issues posed by any interface of wildland and human development.

The route is well marked and easy to follow, even if trail markers have toppled out of their rock cairn bases. It begins as a singletrack linking the boardwalks along the lakeshore, then widens to ranch road beyond the second gate. The trail narrows to singletrack again as it weaves through the grasslands at the southeastern reach of the loop. This section can be overgrown, but it is still easy to follow. The final stretch follows a ranch road along a ruler-straight fenceline to the start of the loop.

Miles and Directions

0.0 Start at the information board at the northeast corner of the parking lot.

0.2 The trail winds along the lakeshore, crossing the second of many boardwalks that curve over seasonal streams.

0.7 Cross a wooden bridge.

1.0 Cross a twin set of bridges.

1.1 Reach a ranch road and gate. Pass through the gate (be sure to close it behind you) onto the obvious singletrack trail. Views grow Montana-big across grasslands, stretching eastward to the distant Sierra.

1.4 Cross a bridge over a gentle depression in the range. This is vernal pool territory in winter and spring, with water swelling to fill low spots. When dry, rocks litter pockets in the fields.

1.7 Odd, orderly hummocks pop from the prairie to the east as you cross another bridge and approach a fenceline and gate.

1.8 Pass through the gate, closing it behind you, and turn right (south) onto the ranch road. The hummocks grow taller, on your left (east) as you proceed. You can't see what's on the other side, but the presence of trees indicates there might be a pond or watering hole.

2.0 Arrive at the start of the loop. You can go in either direction, but it is described clockwise here. Turn left (east) on the trail, headed toward the mountains.

2.1 Cross the first of a series of small bridges spanning seasonal streams that feed man-made ponds on the left (north).

2.5 The trail swings south at a fenceline. More rugged now, the track and the landscape show little sign of human handiwork.

2.8 The trail curves west through a huge swale. What you forgot about as you headed east—the Rancho Seco cooling towers—now pop in and out of view. You are on high ground: The prairie drops to the southeast, dotted with cattle, fences, and ponds. The sometimes-thin track swoops through several more broad ravines, overlooking the pastoral scene as it proceeds south and west.

3.9 Reach a fenceline and trail marker at a ranch road and turn right (north).

4.3 Veer away from the fence on the roadway, still headed north, and pass a trail marker.

4.5 Pass through an area that may be mucky when wet. The road returns to the fenceline. During the spring, these precious vernal pools provide habitat for rare and endangered invertebrates and wildflowers. Stay on the trail to avoid disrupting the pools.

4.9 Reach the trail junction at the start of the loop. Stay straight (north) on the ranch road, retracing your steps to the trailhead.

6.9 Arrive back at the trailhead and parking area.

Appendix: Day Hiker Checklist

Use this list or create your own, based on the nature of your hike and personal needs.

Clothing

- ☐ hat
- ☐ fleece jacket
- ☐ rain gear
- ☐ swimsuit
- ☐ extra socks

Footwear

- ☐ comfortable hiking boots
- ☐ water shoes or sandals

Food and Drink

- ☐ trail mix
- ☐ snacks
- ☐ water

Photography

- ☐ camera
- ☐ film
- ☐ accessories
- ☐ dry bag

Navigation

- ☐ maps
- ☐ compass
- ☐ GPS unit

Miscellaneous

- ☐ pedometer
- ☐ binoculars
- ☐ watch
- ☐ daypack
- ☐ sunglasses
- ☐ sunscreen
- ☐ insect repellent
- ☐ first-aid kit
- ☐ toilet paper
- ☐ small trowel or shovel
- ☐ extra plastic bags to pack out trash
- ☐ flashlight
- ☐ batteries
- ☐ knife/multipurpose tool
- ☐ matches in waterproof container and fire starter
- ☐ this hiking guide

About the Author

Tracy Salcedo-Chourré has written more than a dozen guidebooks to destination in Colorado and California, including *Hiking Lassen Volcanic National Park, Exploring California's Missions and Presidios, Exploring Point Reyes National Seashore and the Golden Gate National Recreation Area,* and *Best Easy Day Hikes* guides to Denver, Boulder, Aspen, Lake Tahoe, the San Francisco Peninsula, San Francisco's East Bay, and San Jose.

She is also an editor, teacher, and soccer mom—and still finds time to hike, cycle, swim, and ski. She lives with her husband, three sons, and small menagerie of pets in California's wine country.

What's So Special about Unspoiled, Natural Places?

Beauty   Solitude   Wildness   Freedom   Quiet   Adventure
Serenity   Inspiration   Wonder   Excitement
Relaxation   Challenge

There's a lot to love about our treasured public lands, and the reasons are different for each of us. Whatever your reasons are, the national **Leave No Trace** education program will help you discover special outdoor places, enjoy them, and preserve them—today and for those who follow. By practicing and passing along these simple principles, you can help protect the special places you love from being loved to death.

The Principles of Leave No Trace

- Plan ahead and prepare
- Travel and camp on durable surfaces
- Dispose of waste properly
- Leave what you find
- Minimize campfire impacts
- Respect wildlife
- Be considerate of other visitors